For Sandra, littl

Penguin

The 12 Secrets of Health and Happiness

Louise Samways is a bestselling author, clinical psychologist in private practice, and professional speaker. She is also the author of *The Chemical Connection*, *The Non-toxic House*, *Your Mindbody Energy* and *Dangerous Persuaders*. Married for twenty-five years, she lives with her family on the Mornington Peninsula in Victoria, Australia.

Be not the slave of your own past ~
plunge into the sublime seas,
dive deep, and swim far,
so you shall come back
with self-respect, with new power,
with an advanced experience,
that shall explain and overlook
the old.
(Ralph Waldo Emerson)

To my husband and children for their loving support and for the fun and joy they bring to my life.

To all my patients who have taught me about the extraordinary capacity of people to be happy and to feel healthy despite overwhelming tragedy and serious illness.

To Ray McLean, who interpreted the illustration brief with such good humour, skill and patience.

The 12
Secrets of
Health and
Happiness

LOUISE
SAMWAYS

Penguin Books

Penguin Books Australia Ltd
487 Maroondah Highway, PO Box 257
Ringwood, Victoria 3134, Australia
Penguin Books Ltd
Harmondsworth, Middlesex, England
Viking Penguin, A Division of Penguin Books USA Inc.
375 Hudson Street, New York, New York 10014, USA
Penguin Books Canada Limited
10 Alcorn Avenue, Toronto, Ontario, Canada M4V 3B2
Penguin Books (N.Z.) Ltd
Cnr Rosedale and Airborne Roads, Albany, Auckland, New
Zealand

First published by Penguin Books Australia Ltd 1997

10 9 8 7 6 5 4 3 2

Illustrations by Ray McLean
Diagrams by Kim Roberts
Typeset in 13pt Centaur by Midland Typesetters,
Maryborough, Victoria
Printed in Australia by Australian Print Group,
Maryborough, Victoria

National Library of Australia
Cataloguing-in-Publication data

Samways, Louise, 1951– .
    The 12 secrets of health and happiness.

    Bibliography.
    ISBN 0 14 026591 0.

    1. Happiness. 2. Mind and body. I. Title. II. Title:
    Twelve secrets of health and happiness.

Contents

PART TWO 🖎

Secrets of Happy People 67

Introduction: The intriguing nature of health and happiness

'By your late twenties you will be a respiratory cripple dependent on oxygen, and you will probably die by your mid-thirties. You may be lucky and reach forty.'

After months of tests and deteriorating health I had insisted on some straight answers.

I was nineteen, in love and very happy. The specialist may have been talking about my body, but he was not talking about me. I got a few more opinions; they all said much the same thing. In many ways I was relieved: being dead at forty was a long way off. It certainly allayed my fears that how awful I felt meant I was on the way out now.

I visited the hospital pharmacy, and emerged with a shopping bag full of six months' supply of various medications, some of them experimental with ghastly side effects. I tried them all and then flushed them down the toilet. I ignored notices of appointments for more tests. (I don't advocate this course to others, but at

nineteen that's what I did.) As far as I was concerned my lungs might be sick but *I* wasn't, so my body would just have to tag along with what I wanted to do.

The following years are a bit of a blur. I continued studying and working. That meant ruthlessly prioritising everything. I would get home and immediately fall into bed, where I stayed until I dragged myself up the next morning. Weekends were for recovery and preparing for the next week. There was no energy for a social life, but I was still very happy.

I never queried or anguished over my unusual lifestyle; it was simply what I had to do. I loved teaching but it was physically too hard for me, so I began clinical training as a psychologist.

'You have nerve deafness. Your hearing is deteriorating rapidly. You'll never work as a psychologist.'

'But I like this work.'

More expert opinions. All the same result. I finally convinced myself the hearing tests were the problem and my tinnitus just confused the tests. To supplement the hearing I still had I learnt to lip-read and continued training as a psychologist. Hearing aids just made the deafness louder and reminded me I had a hearing problem, so it was best not to use them. I was enjoying my work and was very happy.

'You should not have children.'

'But I want children so much. Everywhere I look I see pregnant women, prams and babies.'

Then years of trying.

An internationally respected gynaecologist: 'Your Fallopian tubes are completely blocked. Because of your lungs the anaesthetists refuse to allow elective surgery to unblock them. They are so badly damaged surgery probably wouldn't help anyway.'

No surgery.

I got pregnant. Twice. I had two children. The most wonderful and joyful time of my life. Physical health not too good. I am very happy. Hearing worse.

More difficult working as a psychologist.

'You'll have to give it up!'

I started writing. Great fun and a new challenge. Fortieth birthday! Not dead yet! Still working as a psychologist, and I'm now forty-five.

Even when I have been in hospital with my body feeling very sick I have never thought of myself as a sick person. And even though in my adult life I have grieved deeply for many relatives and close and cherished friends who have died suddenly or slowly, and have known the despair of depression induced by illness, I have seen my life as being happy and fortunate.

My story is by no means unique. People who believe they are healthy can better predict their morbidity than can their doctors.

So what is health and happiness?

Strangely enough, health and happiness appear to have little to do with what's actually happening in your life or in your body. So long as basic needs for safety and comfort are met, and you are not being physically or emotionally threatened by other people, you can feel healthy and happy.

I have seen many people close to death who have said that although they are not happy to die, they feel peaceful and happy. Others living with chronic and debilitating illnesses described themselves as well people, while there have been many with enviable physical health and no personal hassles who are miserable.

> ◊ So long as basic needs for safety and comfort are met, and you are not being physically or emotionally threatened by other people, you can feel healthy and happy. ◊

Because each of us has a unique perspective on the world, it is better that we each interpret the meaning of happiness and health for ourselves.

Chasing rainbows

The fact that there are no tangible definitions probably explains why the search for health and happiness can become elusive and frustrating, like chasing rainbows or fossicking for gold.

For some it is a ravenous, consuming passion that drains energy and time but also provides a distraction or even a complete escape from other issues too difficult to confront. What is often completely missed is that happiness comes from being involved in doing things. If, however, your attention turns more and more inwards on a fascinating study of your own navel, then friends, family, lots of money and your real self can be lost with no improvement in health or happiness. Worse still, as explained in my previous books *Dangerous Persuaders* and *Your Mindbody Energy*, the seeking in itself can be devastatingly damaging. Personal development is one of the fastest-growing industries of the Western world, worth billions of dollars per year. And yet academics have sadly neglected this human need for health and happiness, and our often anguished search.

> ✎ *What is often completely missed is that happiness comes from being involved in doing things.* ✎

Is happiness abnormal?

Over the last twenty years psychological journals have cited 29 216 studies on depression, 27 244 on anxiety, and 5199 on anger. But in all that time there were only 1664 on happiness, 1207 on life satisfaction and a tiny 614 on joy. Misery studies outnumbered happiness studies 18:1!

With such a heavy emphasis on the study of misery, you could be forgiven for thinking that the people of the world are a very unhappy lot. Doctor Richard Bertall, a clinical psychologist, set psychiatric and psychological academics abuzz with a 'spoof' article in a leading scientific journal in which he used this disproportionate amount of research on misery (you can use statistics to prove anything!) to suggest that happiness was so 'statistically abnormal' that it 'probably reflects the abnormal functioning of the central nervous system'. He went on to propose that perhaps happiness should be declared a psychiatric illness: 'major affective disorder, pleasant type'.

That article got people thinking, and since then there has been a dramatic increase in research by social and health psychologists and sociologists into what makes us happy and healthy. These 'happiologists' or 'subjective wellbeing' experts (trust an academic to come up with a label like that!) are discovering the fascinating secrets of what makes people happy and healthy. Contrary to what you may think, most people *are* happy and reasonably healthy. Happy people tend to be healthier, but chronically ill or disabled people can still feel very happy. And as long as basic needs are being met, money has little to do with the degree of happiness, nor does age or race.

Many, many books are written with an incorrect underlying assumption that a particular stage of life – adolescence, marriage, divorce, parenthood, midlife, menopause, retirement, even life itself – is inherently distressful and causes a high degree of dissatisfaction and unhappiness. But the age or stage of a person's life cannot predict their degree of happiness. People tend to be just as happy at any age or stage.

> The age or stage of a person's life cannot predict their degree of happiness. People tend to be just as happy at any age or stage.

Men and women tend to suffer their misery differently. Although women are more vulnerable to serious depression, men are far more likely to be alcoholics or to have antisocial and personality problems. But when measuring the overall or 'global' level of happiness and unhappiness there is no significant difference between men and women. Surveys show that most women in the Western world appear to be quite happy working part time and making their families a much higher priority than a full-time career. Most women do not seem to need or want a full-time career to feel fulfilled and happy.

In the Western world the pursuit of more money and a higher material standard of living is becoming an obsession of governments and of many individuals that is often at odds with the quality of life. Social factors, lifestyle priorities and values are more important than money in determining how healthy you are.

In America, although national income and what it can buy doubled between the 1950s and the 1990s, surveys asking people how happy they feel have shown no change in the degree of reported happiness.

In other studies of the reported happiness of people in different countries, there has been a significant correlation between the length of time a country has had a democratic government and the degree of life satisfaction: a sense of control over your life and individual freedom is crucial to health and happiness.

Particularly significant is that regardless of life events people tend not to change their degree of reported happiness over ten years. Those that were originally miserable stayed miserable and those that were originally happy stayed happy. People tended to be either chronically miserable or chronically happy!

You can be happy now

If you tend to fall into the trap of thinking 'I'll be happy when ...' or 'I'd be happy if ...', then being happy or happier is always in the future. It is common for people to think and feel that 'I'll be happy when':

> ﹅ If you tend to fall into the trap of thinking 'I'll be happy when ...' or 'I'd be happy if ...', then being happy or happier is always in the future. ﹅

- my debts are cleared
- my health is better
- my marriage improves

- my exams are over
- my kids appreciate me more ...

Or 'I'd be happy if':

- I lost weight
- I was married
- I was more attractive
- I had more friends ...

To be happier you first have to decide to be happier right *now*, this second! Are you prepared to allow yourself to be happy *now*? Do you feel you deserve to be happy *now*? Probably the greatest inhibitor of feeling good is the kind of thinking that is focused on the past or on the future: what has happened; what could have happened; what might happen; what will happen. You will never be happy or happier if you think you 'have to have all the answers'.

> ✒ To be happier you first have to decide to be happier right now, this second! Are you prepared to allow yourself to be happy now? Do you feel you deserve to be happy now? ✒

As an experiment just see how much happier you are prepared to allow yourself to be by focusing on *this second* of your life. Allow yourself to really experience *this second* with all your senses: what can you see? hear? feel? By allowing yourself to focus more on this moment in time you'll realise that most moments can be very pleasant. And these can become most minutes and most hours.

The Happiness Cake

One of the most common things that can prevent people from letting themselves be happy right now is an underlying belief that happiness is like a cake with only a finite number of portions available. This belief leads to thoughts such as:

- 'If I'm happy now there won't be any happiness left for later.'
- 'If you're happy, there won't be enough happiness left for me.'

If you are frightened that there isn't enough happiness to go around, you may be the kind of person who either deliberately or unconsciously sabotages other people's pleasure:

- 'My son just won the local tennis club tournament.'
  'Oh really? My nephew is state champion.'
- 'Harry just got a wonderful new job. It's so exciting. We're off to live in Paris!'
  'Isn't that where they have all those bomb scares?'

Happiness is like love. It expands to fill the space *you* make available. When you have another child, you don't take love from other people to give to that new baby instead. The love just expands infinitely. Start thinking of happiness as being infinite with plenty to go around for all those who want it, and you will immediately allow yourself and others to be happy right now.

Mind over matter

The type of thinking you allow yourself to indulge in involves one of the most crucial secrets being revealed about happy, healthy people. Not only are your emotions and feelings determined largely by your thoughts, but the remarkable and profound effects of thoughts on the physical body are only beginning to be properly understood.

Try these experiments on yourself:

- Imagine cutting six very juicy lemons, squeezing every last drop of the sour juice and putting it into a glass. Now imagine you are drinking that very sour juice. What do you notice has happened in your mouth? Copious amounts of saliva begin to flow; you may grimace with the muscles of your mouth, neck and shoulders. Merely thinking about some lemons has created psychological, biochemical and muscle changes in your body!

- Think of the most embarrassing moment in your life. Can you feel yourself blushing?

- Imagine sitting in school. The teacher 'squeaks' a piece of chalk across the blackboard. This simple thought runs shivers up and down your spine.

- Imagine sitting naked in a bath full of iced water with ice blocks bobbing around you. Your whole body starts to shiver with this thought!
- Now imagine a nice deep, warm bath, just the right temperature. You feel warmer already.

These little fantasies show how much your thoughts can affect your physical body and your feelings.

Blind positive thinking is not the answer!

Blind positive thinking will not make you genuinely happier. It is deliciously seductive because it promotes a denial of the limitations of individuals' control over their lives. This can produce a wonderful and euphoric anaesthesia, protecting a person from reality. 'You can be anything you want to be'; 'If you are sick, it's because you want to be sick'. While a little bit of denial can be very healthy, too much can distort perceptions to the extent where individuals can no longer function effectively in the world the way it really is. Such people often start to withdraw or join groups with similar delusions. As the conflict between their distorted perceptions and the real world becomes too painful and too difficult to manage, their isolation increases, in

> While a little bit of denial can be very healthy, too much can distort perceptions to the extent where individuals can no longer function effectively in the world the way it really is.

some cases leading to serious emotional problems or psychoses.

The mindbody connection

Thoughts, the emotions they create, and other psychological and social factors have been found to affect the outcome and course of every major disease: cancer, kidney disease, gastrointestinal illness, rheumatoid conditions, neurological illness and lung disease.

The great news is that you can be healthier if you learn to change, and to control, your feelings and physical reactions. To do this you must not deny the way you feel but instead recognise and acknowledge your situation and your reactions to it realistically. But remember to remain aware of the present and future consequences of your actions. You can then go on to choose to develop appropriate self-talk, which empowers you and maximises your ability to cope and your own natural healing response.

So why are some people happier and healthier than others?

What are their secrets?

Read on. You are about to find out!

PART ONE

Unlocking the
Secrets of Health and
Happiness

The chain and its links

Many studies have explored the connection between thoughts, feelings and actions. For our purposes let us make the starting point of this chain reaction our perceptions of events in our lives, which create underlying beliefs about ourselves and the world around us. The creation and development of a set

> ❧ The creation and development of a set of beliefs are vital to every aspect of human functioning. ❧

of beliefs are vital to every aspect of human functioning. If we didn't develop a consistent set of beliefs, every event would be newly encountered; we could not learn from experience and there would be no level of predictability in our lives. We would all be nervous wrecks with no idea of what might happen next.

In order to use the secrets discovered about healthy and happy people, you need to be aware of the chain reaction connecting thoughts and feelings so that you can control and manipulate each link in the chain.

16

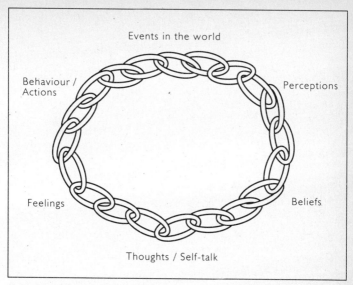

Events in the world

Behaviour /
Actions

Perceptions

Feelings

Beliefs

Thoughts / Self-talk

The chain

Awareness and control of each link is even more important when you realise that the chain is linked in a circle. So making mistakes tends to lead to more misery, leading to more mistakes and more misery ... a truly vicious circle! Getting it right leads to feeling good, which leads to getting it right even more and feeling even better – an empowering and exciting cycle of good feelings and experiences.

As a young child you may experience (event) a number of adults being cross with you (perception), so you develop a belief that you make adults cross (belief). This results in your thinking that you are bad or naughty (self-talk). In turn you feel unhappy, confused and angry because it's not your fault (feelings). Your behaviour becomes difficult and deliberately naughty to provoke the adults who are cross with you (behaviour and actions). The adults get crosser! Your perceptions are confirmed and so the vicious negative cycle continues.

Alternatively, imagine you are a young child experiencing kind and loving adults with plenty of time, energy and patience (event). You see adults as rewarding people to be around (perception) and believe that since they are nice to you they like you. This lets you develop the idea that you are lovable (belief) and you think good things about yourself (thoughts), arousing lots of positive feelings. The good feelings generated by being around adults lead to co-operative behaviour, which makes the adults even more kind and loving, confirming your original perceptions and so a wonderfully positive cycle feeds itself, getting stronger and stronger.

> Although we can dramatically influence events and experiences in our lives we can't totally control them. But we can learn to take extraordinary control of our perceptions, beliefs, thoughts, feelings and actions.

Unfortunately, although we can dramatically influence events and experiences in our lives we can't totally control them. But we can learn to take extraordinary control of our perceptions, beliefs, thoughts, feelings and actions. By becoming aware of these links in the chain, then deliberately manipulating them for positive outcomes, we are using the basic tools necessary to put into practice the secrets of healthier and happier people. Just knowing their secrets isn't much help. Controlling the chain is the key to unlocking each secret and making it work for you.

Events and experiences: Things just happen!

Whether we like to face it or not, the uncomfortable truth is we cannot control everything that happens in our lives. However, we can choose how we are going to perceive or read these events. Perhaps one of the most significant features of an event is how large or small we choose to make it: cataclysmically huge or a mere blip.

With a sudden thud the engine died and all that we could hear was gurgling floodwater rushing into the truck and around our feet. Without thinking, my sister shoved the matches from the glove box inside her bra and I grabbed the single-burner gas stove just as the water level almost reached the window. Quickly we (husband John, brother Greg, sister Charmaine and dog Rufus) scrambled onto the bonnet of the truck as the rushing water rose higher and higher.

We had been caught by an eight-year drought breaking (in the dry season) on a little-used outback track between Oodnadatta and Maree in the gibber desert of South Australia.

The night before, we had camped at the top of a thirty-foot embankment down to a perfectly dry river bed. The torrential rain had started at midnight and, realising how quickly this land could turn from never-ending desert to never-ending water, we had broken camp and sat in the truck anxiously waiting for first light so we could make a dash out of the area. It was too dangerous to travel in the dark because it was too easy to miss the vague track and drive off into the desert.

As we moved off with the first inkling of a grey dawn, we saw only water; the previously dry riverbed was nearly breaking its banks. In four-wheel drive we ground our way along through constant water. Every now and then we reached a depression indicating a water course. With no way of telling depth, we'd take a run and plough through the raging creeks now merging across the desert. But after fifty kilometres, countless such crossings, continual blinding rain and visibility of only a few yards, our luck ran out and the truck fell into a wash-out in a creekbed.

Using the winch cable and rope, we tied ourselves to a lifeline and waded and swam out of the creekbed into shallower water, using the desert mulga to stop ourselves being washed away.

The grey sky and water merged as we struggled onto a mound of dry ground no more than ten feet in diameter. Shocked and shivering uncontrollably, we realised we had to find shelter somewhere in this sea of water.

Where we stood seemed fairly safe for the moment so we lit the gas stove and piled sopping mulga over it. Somehow we got a fire going which, while it cheered us, didn't warm us. The chill factor from the wind made the rain feel as if it came straight from Antarctica. We later found out a depression coming from Antarctica was actually the reason for the weird weather in the dry season.

Realising we couldn't stay long where we were, we pitched a hiker's tent rescued from the truck. As I was the coldest I stayed put with Rufus, piling on mulga while the others went to look for higher ground.

We moved fire and tent to higher ground five times that day as the water continued to rise with the incessant rain and the wind cutting us like a knife.

Perceptions:
Interpreting what has happened

That night we all squashed into the single hiker's tent with Rufus and shivered until a bleak but rainless dawn. As the desert was rocky shingle we couldn't get a tent peg into the ground, so the guy ropes had to be held down by piles of rocks. Periodically in the night a rope would come loose and I thankfully let the men go out in the cold to fix it. It was no time to be a feminist.

We were too cold to sleep so we talked. To my amazement John and Greg were planning rescuing the truck. They discussed for hours the effects of water, mud and silt on every working part: gearbox, engine, wheels, brakes, and so on. It didn't enter their heads to worry about our very dangerous position.

Charmaine started longing for a cigarette and wondered if she could rescue some soggy ones from the truck, then dry them in front of the fire on a grid made from mulga twigs. She talked incessantly about what provisions we had and how they could be dried and what interesting food we could create. She held absolutely no thoughts of despair. Rufus was obviously hungry, but he was happy as long as he was in the middle of us all.

I was just scared stiff and painfully obsessed with the rocks sticking into my bottom. I decided I was so cold I could easily roll over and go to sleep permanently and not care. I was the only one who had read about flash floods in the desert and how unsuspecting travellers could be washed away by three-metre walls of water that came from thousands of kilometres away in northern Queensland. With a shock I realised I was a wimp in a crisis.

We were all in the same mess but our respective perceptions of our position varied according to our beliefs about ourselves, our priorities and our knowledge.

These were rather extreme circumstances to have to deal with but some people forget that, as human beings, we have been designed to adapt to and cope with all kinds of negative situations, even quite dangerous or unhappy ones.

> 🖎 We were all in the same mess but our respective perceptions of our position varied according to our beliefs about ourselves, our priorities and our knowledge. 🖎

Marooned as we were in the desert, we depended for survival on quickly and accurately perceiving the situation so we could mobilise our energy constructively towards survival. While John, Greg and Charmaine focused on what they could do now, I focused on my discomfort and what might happen in the future.

SUSAN AND NEIL – A CASE STUDY

Susan and Neil were in a self-help group for parents of brain damaged children. Their eight-year-old son Jack had recently survived an accident in which he was knocked off his bike while riding to school. He was now severely brain damaged. Susan and Neil were both the least educated and sophisticated parents in the group, but their intuitive wisdom and insight were remarkable. While the other parents were understandably suffering obvious and varying degrees of distress, anguish and desperation, Susan and Neil calmly talked about Jack's rehabilitation and how they would manage when he came home from hospital.

After a few sessions I was beginning to wonder whether their apparent calmness was in fact a denial of the seriousness of Jack's disabilities. But in one particularly difficult session another parent accused them of being heartless as they appeared to be coping so much better than the other parents. Their accuser was an enormously successful businessman who was used to being able to control or remove obstacles or people who got in his way.

At this attack, Susan and Neil instinctively reached out to hold each other's hand. Very quietly, and with tears welling in his eyes, Neil explained that they were grieving deeply for the loss of Jack who they felt had 'died' on the day of the accident. They regarded the Jack they now had as being 'born' on that day, and that this new son was someone they had to get to know and love.

To Susan and Neil, the two Jacks were like twins, identical but different. Unlike the other parents, they were allowing themselves to fully grieve Jack 'One'. To help themselves, the family had already held a very private memorial service for Jack 'One' so that they could move on to loving Jack 'Two'. By grieving for Jack 'One', Susan and Neil were not as tortured by the comparisons between a pre- and post-accident Jack.

Initially the other parents were shocked by Susan and Neil's way of coping, but over the next few weeks they all said their own anguish had become more manageable as soon as they had accepted that the child they had known had 'died', and that a disabled twin had been 'born'.

Some people seem to know the trick of keeping an appropriate perspective and deliberately choosing the easiest and most expedient way of dealing with things. Good copers don't create anguish within themselves by distorting the size of the problem or by fighting it. They simply acknowledge its existence and put their energy into finding a solution.

For other people, things that don't go their way become huge mountains to be scaled. They'd never dream of taking the easy way by walking around the mountain or even away in the opposite direction! No, everything has to be a looming cliff face to be battled head-on. Alternatively they rail against fate and fight the situation. Their anguish leaves little energy to do what is necessary or to think clearly.

The emotional and physical impact of even very serious events can be dramatically affected by how a person chooses to perceive them. Many of the people I see have terminal illnesses or are receiving lengthy, time-consuming and distressingly uncomfortable treatment. Cancer patients particularly can find their whole lives and those of their families quickly dominated by their illness and its treatment. Many complain that the treatment is far more intrusive and difficult to deal with than the illness itself.

However, perceptions can become very distorted because patients start to spend so much time thinking about the illness and treatment and the anticipation of their discomfort. When they keep a diary of the actual time spent on treatment, excluding the thinking time, they are often amazed at how much less it is than they thought.

Similarly, students can moan and complain about how much work they are doing but again a diary can reveal the reality that more time is being spent thinking about studying than actually doing it.

By focusing on actual time and leaving thinking time free to experience other things in life, in other words by focusing on the moment rather than on what has happened or what will happen, you can suddenly discover a whole lot more living time and the chore or hassle ceases to encompass your life. Here is a useful trick to help you cope with all kinds of unfortunate events or things in your life you don't like. Imagine yourself looking at a giant screen filled with all the things happening to you at that time, including the mundane, the habitual, the good, the not-so-good and the downright unpleasant. So the screen is filled with *everything*.

Now imagine you have a telescope. If you look through a telescope one way you can adjust it to make things look bigger so that the entire visual field is filled with just one object or incident on the screen. However, if you look through the telescope from the opposite end you can adjust the focus so that the same incident or object can almost disappear as the visual field is filled with the total picture.

> ✒ By focusing on the moment rather than on what has happened or what will happen, you can suddenly discover a whole lot more living time. ✒

You can practise now with something you don't like. Perhaps your nose. Imagine a picture of yourself on a very large screen doing everyday things: going to work, playing sport, participating in a hobby, being alone, doing the dishes, cleaning your teeth ... As you watch yourself, take the telescope and adjust it so your nose fills the entire visual field; you can see nothing but nose. Yuk! Nobody's nose looks good close up. Now take the telescope and look through it from the other end and look at the screen. Now your nose is so small compared with everything else you can hardly see it!

Changing your perspective changes what you see.

The same trick can be used with what you hear. Imagine you have a volume control or a sound filter. You can now choose how much you hear and what you hear. (This is often called selective deafness, a very handy trick for parents – and their children!) What you hear can also be dramatically affected by what you believe about yourself or about the person talking. If you like yourself and think the other person does too, you will tend to look for language, tone of voice and non-verbal behaviour that confirms this belief. Even if you are actually being criticised, you will try to rationalise it as not really being the way the person feels.

If you are uncertain of yourself and don't like the other person much, you tend to magnify the significance of tone of voice and non-verbal language, interpreting what is said in a very negative way to reaffirm your own negative beliefs.

Beliefs

Our beliefs about ourselves and about the world around us develop over many years. In childhood we are physiologically and psychologically designed to acquire beliefs and modify them more easily than adults. Once acquired, beliefs that have been consolidated in adulthood are difficult to change, although they can be modified.

A very significant event which dramatically increases your level of arousal can make beliefs easier to change. An example of this is people who experience a religious conversion after serious illness or bereavement. There are also a number of persuasive techniques widely used in the community to deliberately manipulate and modify beliefs.

Except for religious beliefs, most of our beliefs are unconscious. We are not usually aware of them or of how much they are influencing our thinking. For instance, it has been common for women to be brought up to see their own needs as less important than those of other family members. Unless they are aware of this belief many women find themselves constantly giving in to others to their own detriment, angry with themselves for being 'doormats' but unaware of why they continue to allow it to happen. Once they are aware of the underlying belief, they can choose to modify it to be something more appropriate for the way they now want to be. Believing they have equal rights and demanding that their needs also be respected changes their behaviour.

CASSIE – A CASE STUDY

Cassie was thirty-five, single and extremely lonely. She'd read many books on being happily single and knew all the things to do to get people in her life. But somehow she could never get past casual acquaintanceship with anyone. There were lots of people in her life but there was no intimacy.

As we explored how long Cassie had felt this way, it became clear that her natural shyness had led to a protective belief that 'I don't belong'. If she believed she didn't belong she didn't have to confront her fear of people.

Once she adopted this belief she then made damned sure it became true either by unconsciously avoiding other people's overtures for a more friendly relationship or by attacking and judging people so that they avoided her. But once Cassie became more aware of this underlying belief and why she held onto it, we could begin to face the issue of her wariness and distrust of people.

She realised that her wariness might have been entirely appropriate as a small child but that as an adult she had other skills that could protect her. It wasn't long before she felt confident enough to believe 'I can now belong'. This change in belief about herself changed her feelings and her behaviour. She no longer found fault with everyone and there was no need to avoid other people's friendliness.

Using her new-found 'people skills' she now felt able to handle intimacy.

Core beliefs

Because core beliefs tend to be unconscious, discovering what they are can be very difficult, especially as they generate ways of behaving, attitudes and thinking patterns that can cause you to either maintain, avoid or compensate for them. The underlying core belief can become well and truly hidden behind a life that just doesn't seem to 'click', and can create chronic discontent.

It's not just what happens to us when we are young that affects the development of these core beliefs: genetic and personality factors also come into play. For instance, shy children like Cassie may be at a greater risk of developing a feeling they can't belong than gregarious children, regardless of their experiences or what their parents did or did not do.

So don't start blaming your parents for being the sole cause of your wacky beliefs! In my experience nearly all parents, no matter how inadequate, muddle along as well as they can with the best of intentions, their own inadequacy often feeding from their less-than-perfect backgrounds.

The most common destructive core beliefs are:

'*I don't deserve to be happy, successful, free from pain …*'   If you feel you don't deserve the good things in life, you will act in ways that don't allow you to access or enjoy these good things – even when they fall in your lap! This core belief can be created when people feel guilt as a result of abuse or religious belief, or if they are a member of a minority group that suffers discrimination in the community.

'*My emotional needs will never be met by other people.*'   This can stem from parents who are unable or unwilling to give a child what they need emotionally, for example encouragement, affection, love, nurturing, caring, guidance.

> If you feel you don't deserve the good things in life, you will act in ways that don't allow you to access or enjoy these good things – even when they fall in your lap!

'*You can't rely on close relationships because they don't last.*'   This is common in adults who come from broken homes, who lost a parent through death or who were left alone at home inappropriately for their age.

'*You can't believe people – they'll only hurt you.*'   This belief can lead to defensive barriers being created against intimacy by means of aggression and vindictiveness, for example, or 'pay-back'. It can develop when a child is emotionally, physically or sexually abused by parents, peers, teachers, siblings or carers.

'I can't belong.' This belief can stem from personality factors that make a child timid, shy or self-conscious. It can also stem from experiences of isolation and/or rejection due to real differences in a child's culture, ability or values.

Children who have been abused can be deliberately prevented from becoming intimate with anyone or from belonging to any group outside the family. This ensures the 'family secret' is kept safe. These children can grow up with the core belief that they cannot belong anywhere outside the family.

'There's something wrong with me'; 'I'm inadequate.' Such beliefs can develop where children or adults are in a highly critical, condemning environment where approval is conditional on unrealistic expectations being met.

'I'm not attractive enough to be liked or accepted.' This is extremely common with children and teenagers but can last well into adulthood. It is often based on clearly remembered experiences of being teased and actively rejected by school peers or family because of

some aspect of their appearance, or when the school or family is obsessive about appearances.

People with this belief will often go to extreme lengths to reinforce it by neglecting basic grooming or deliberately choosing unattractive clothing and hair styles. Chronic problems with obesity can be maintained by this underlying belief.

'I'm not capable of achieving as much as other people.'   This can evolve not only from being put down when you are young but also from not being taught how to handle failure and disappointment. Achieving requires perseverance and self-discipline, and these in turn demand the resilience to handle disappointment. People with this belief often don't bother trying, even when they have obvious talent.

> ✎ Achieving requires perseverance and self-discipline, and these in turn demand the resilience to handle disappointment. ✎

'I can't look after myself without help'; 'I can't look after myself on my own.'   These beliefs of being unable to be autonomous, and of being dependent on others to meet basic day-to-day needs, have become an epidemic among many young adults. Keeping children at school longer is commendable but, unless parents actively encourage and promote independence and autonomy

from an early age, young adults can leave school at eighteen without basic emotional and physical survival skills. This dependency makes them anxious and angry and does not prepare them well for adult relationships or for the workplace.

'Living is dangerous.'   A fearful, overanxious parent with poor emotional and practical resources can give a child an exaggerated view of the likelihood of all kinds of catastrophes occurring. The parent's fears stem from another belief: *'If something terrible occurred I couldn't cope.'* People with these beliefs can limit their life experience and take excessive precautions to try to protect themselves.

'I don't know who I am.'   Very sensitive children or those in families that are abusive, over-protective or too controlling may not be encouraged or allowed to develop a strong sense of self as separate from other people. People with this belief tend to be indecisive and easily manipulated. They commonly describe themselves as feeling empty, hollow or like a rudderless ship at sea.

'I must give in to others to be accepted and to avoid unpleasant consequences.'   This belief can stem from a fear of being rejected or hurt by someone else getting angry, and

leads to passive or compliant patterns of operating that deny the person's own needs and feelings. Many people with this belief readily lie to avoid conflict.

'My own needs are not as important as other people's.'   This belief leads to self-sacrificing behaviour that is very common in women. It may be not only social expectations and parenting causing this belief but also the tendency of women to be generally less self-centred in their outlook than men. However, it can also be very powerful in men who, at a young age, have been made inappropriately responsible for their family's welfare through, for example, a parent's death, illness or alcoholism.

'I must not show my feelings.'   This belief inhibits spontaneity in relationships and deprives the person of real intimacy in their lives. There is a fear that sharing feelings will expose vulnerability or cause rejection and embarrassment. This may also be a fear that sharing feelings, especially anger, will unjustifiably upset others. Such beliefs evolve from cultural, community and family expectations.

'No matter what I do it will never be good enough'; *'Status, wealth and power are more important than relationships, health*

and happiness.' I have put these beliefs together because they tend to occur together and are caused by the same kind of upbringing. The family hasn't necessarily fostered these values but the school and social network have. I'm seeing increasing numbers of parents deeply concerned and shocked by discovering that values like these operate in the particular private schools their children attend. They feel torn between what they perceive (often incorrectly) as the educational advantages that these schools are supposed to offer and the price their children may ultimately pay.

'I'm entitled to what I want now regardless of other people's needs.' There are two environments that tend to develop this self-centred belief. The first is a home or school environment that overindulges children and gives them a feeling of entitlement and superiority over others. The other is an environment in which a child has been socially rejected and/or emotionally deprived, forcing the child to give up on relationships and pursue self-esteem and satisfaction in material rewards.

'I can do what I want when I want.' If your upbringing fails to teach you self-control or how to handle frustration, you are likely to believe this to varying

degrees. In extreme cases this belief can lead to criminal and addictive behaviour.

If you suspect you have other destructive beliefs, one of the most revealing ways to discover them is to write down all the things you think you and other people *should* and *should not* do.

Rules

The exercise described above will reveal the underlying rules you apply to yourself and to others which, if unrealistic or unreasonable, can make you and those you live with very miserable. For example, I should:

- be tidier
- be more punctual
- eat less
- remember everyone's birthday
- not get angry ...

Or he or she should:

- appreciate me more
- keep their room clean to my standards
- drink less alcohol
- stop smoking
- understand me
- not upset me
- do as I say ...

JACK AND MARY – TWO CASE STUDIES

Jack was five and rather shy. In the classroom he was quite attentive and adored his teacher, who made him feel very comfortable. In class there was always someone to talk to or to work with, so he never felt left out or lonely.

But the schoolyard was different. The rowdy unpredictability of so many children left him confused and frightened. His timidity often isolated him even from his own school friends. Being alone and not having anyone to be with seemed the most appalling social sin, even though he was not actively rejected. Jack's rule said: 'I *should* always have someone to play with'.

As he sat on my knee and sobbed his heart out he could only hiccup his distress to me until I hugged him and said, 'Oh, but hasn't anyone told you! You don't *have* to have someone to play with at school. You can play on your own and I'll show you how.'

Jack stopped sobbing and looked at me, wide-eyed. His shoulders relaxed and his little body slowly stopped quivering. Soon he was joining in making a list of all the things he could have in his bag in case he wanted to play on his own: a bat and ball, marbles, cards to play patience, chalk to draw on the asphalt, and so on.

And, of course, as soon as the other children saw him happy on his own they wanted to play with him too!

Mary was the eldest and had grown up in a migrant family from southern Europe. Her parents had each worked two jobs to support their brood of six children. At thirteen Mary disappeared from school to look after the younger children and help her mother meet the sewing deadlines of her contract work at home.

She dearly loved and respected her parents but, hearing the constant stories of their hardship in their home country and the unrelenting work in their new country, she came to believe that even as an adult she had no right to any leisure time and that life meant continual self-sacrifice and exhaustion.

Even when she married a successful businessman she was still driven to create work for herself and felt panicky and irritable if he insisted on some leisure time. Mary's rule said: 'Good mothers and fathers suffer and sacrifice themselves for their children'.

When she came to me she realised she had no reason to work so hard now, but she was riddled with a guilty feeling that by not working she was betraying the values and suffering of her parents.

Mary could never allow herself to enjoy parenthood and life generally until she changed the rules in her head.

Rules can be helpful guides to living but they can also trigger despair and guilt when they are broken. If you have too many rules in your life, check that they are realistic and reasonable.

Guilt

If you are plagued by guilt, look at the underlying rule you think you have broken and ask yourself whether it is appropriate for this time of your life. Many rules that were entirely appropriate for childhood, your parents' era and even another stage of your own life can be plain dangerous and provoke unnecessary guilt at other times. Maybe the rule merely needs to be updated to fit your current life situation.

> ✎ Rules can be helpful guides to living but they can also trigger despair and guilt when they are broken. ✎

Instilling a rule in children that they should always do what adults tell them to can put them in dangerous situations if approached by child molesters, be they relatives, acquaintances or complete strangers.

Someone brought up to believe that marriage is always forever will suffer far more if their marriage breaks down than those who will try to make it work but realise that in fact marriages often don't.

Men and women who believe they should always try to please their partner can be in for a miserable guilt-ridden existence if their partner takes advantage of their self-sacrificing behaviour.

Men and women who believe that masturbation is taboo miss out on the delights of different kinds of sexual pleasure once they are married or have a partner. Masturbating or making love to your partner is like choosing between an apple and a banana. Sometimes you just like something different.

Although becoming aware of unhelpful and damaging beliefs is important, it is just as important to be aware of healthier and more helpful alternatives. You might like to consider adopting the following beliefs.

Seven beliefs to make you happier

1. I am a human being and as a human being I have a right to make mistakes (even catastrophic ones). It means I'm human, not bad. I have a right to have strengths and weaknesses. Nobody else expects me to be perfect, so why should I?

2. I like to be loved, appreciated, respected and approved of but I can't expect to have the whole world think of me like that or even all the people I know. Their approval is good but I do not have to depend on it to be happy.

3. Other people or situations can't make me unhappy; it is what I tell myself that determines how I feel. For example, if someone criticises my clothes I

can choose to let that upset me or I can choose to ignore it.

4. I am responsible for making my own happiness but I am not responsible for making other people happy. Nor am I responsible for other people's problems. I am, however, responsible for my behaviour towards other people, especially children.

5. While unhappy, sad or traumatic things may have happened to me in the past, they don't have to devastate my future. I can let go of feelings about those unhappy times.

6. No matter what life throws at me, I know I can cope alone if necessary. I may not like what happens but as a human being I have been designed to cope with good and bad, happy and sad, and to survive! If I am anguished it is because I am fighting the situation. If I accept it I will have the strength and energy to deal with it.

7. I am allowed to feel anxious, frightened or unsure.

These are human emotions in certain situations and *I am human.*

Such beliefs acknowledge you as a human being with a full range of strengths and weaknesses, and the right to feel a complete range of emotions. Combine these beliefs with a strong sense of your own ability to tap into the resources necessary for dealing with whatever arises (even if you don't like it), and you will be well equipped to access the secrets of being happier and healthier and to have empowering thoughts or self-talk.

Self-talk: Controlling the CDs playing in your head

Thinking is really like an internal dialogue with yourself. It is perfectly normal for it to seem like voices in your head telling you things from different perspectives.

One day a worried mum brought her four-year-old son to me. He had started to talk about the voices in his head that 'wouldn't shut up'. Finally I realised it was his thinking he was 'hearing'. This internal talking or self-talk plays a vital role in our interpretation of events and how we choose to respond.

FRANK – A CASE STUDY

Some years ago an eleven-year-old boy called Frank was referred to me by his local school. Frank had been expelled from three private schools and now had a full-time minder employed by a State education department to sit next to him in class and follow him around the school grounds to stop him attacking other students or teachers. Numerous psychiatrists and psychologists had seen him and his family, and his file with the State's community services department was thirty centimetres thick.

> ✐ Thinking is really like an internal dialogue with yourself. It is perfectly normal for it to seem like voices in your head telling you things from different perspectives. ✐

He arrived for his appointment sullen and dressed in cut-down army fatigues and heavy boots. Sitting with his arms crossed, he became very cocky when I asked him to explain what event had resulted in his throwing a chair at the teacher and putting a fellow student in hospital with head injuries.

'They made me do it,' was his explanation. 'The teacher told me to stop talking and I didn't want to.

'That kid [the one now in hospital] said he wouldn't play marbles with me because I cheat.'

I asked him why he gave other people so much power and if he was happy letting other people have such fantastic control over him. At first he looked as if he would explode with rage but then he looked puzzled and asked me what on earth I meant.

This boy had never been shown that he had choices over his reactions to events and that these choices determined whether he was in control or whether someone else could push his buttons and control his reactions.

He soon realised that other people were controlling him more and more as the rest of the students realised what good sport it was to goad him. This idea appalled him and even in that first session he was intrigued to know about other ways of reacting that would put *him* in control.

It had never occurred to him that if you were teased you weren't compelled to react violently. He soon learnt that being teased was a nuisance but that depending on the self-talk he chose he could control how he felt about the teasing and what he did about it. To his surprise, he found he felt infinitely stronger (and more superior!) when he ignored teasing rather than when he let himself froth at the mouth with rage, and attack.

As you will see on pages 68–70, a good style of self-talk does not mean blind positive thinking, which denies your reactions, needs or reality. For instance, it is not helpful to say to yourself 'every day in every way I am getting better and better' when in the bathroom mirror each morning you can see yourself wasting away from cancer. And it can be sheer hell for family and friends if nobody is allowed to openly discuss the reality of the situation.

One of my patients was absolutely besotted with New Age beliefs and healing practices. She believed that because she didn't want to be ill she could never get sick. Regardless of a family history of breast cancer – her mother, grandmother, aunt and two sisters had died of breast cancer – she refused to have mammograms or examine her own breasts. When she was diagnosed with advanced metastatic breast cancer, her whole belief system was shattered and she was left to die in extreme anger, confusion and anguish.

There are ten very common types of distorted or wacky thinking practices that we all use to varying degrees. They underlie many of our inappropriate negative feelings.

Cognitive distortions

David Burns, in his book *Feeling Good* (invaluable for a comprehensive understanding of thoughts and moods), categorises ten main kinds of *cognitive distortions*:

1. **All or nothing thinking**
People who habitually use this kind of thinking see

things in black or white. They cannot cope with the grey. Unfortunately for them, most things in life are grey.

Their own personal qualities are seen as all bad or all good. One mistake means they are helpless failures; anything not as it 'should be' is a disaster. This kind of thinking leads to obsessive perfectionism where they cannot be comfortable if everything is not the way they think it ought to be. One thing out of place and the house is a mess. One hair out of place and they are sloppy.

But if you look around you will realise that life rarely fits the extremes of all bad or all good and that we can easily develop personally distorted perceptions of what defines clean, tidy, good, bad, ugly or beautiful.

2. **Overgeneralising**

If you fear rejection and avoid putting yourself in situations where you could be rejected, you may be overgeneralising from when something unpleasant has happened. For instance, if you miss out on a job application and then say to yourself 'I'll never get a job' you are overgeneralising from one particular incident to always. Or if you forget your wife's birthday you might say 'My memory is hopeless'. An over-generalising student is prone to say 'I failed that maths test so I'm hopeless at maths'.

It's very important not to globalise individual negative events. Instead acknowledge the unpleasantness of a specific incident that is now over and move on. For example:

It's very important not to globalise individual negative events. Instead acknowledge the unpleasantness of a specific incident that is now over and move on.

- 'I didn't get *that* job.'
- 'I forgot my wife's birthday *this* year.'
- 'I failed *that* maths test so I'll study harder for the next.'

3. Using mental filters

You may have heard of people who look at everything through rose-tinted glasses. Well, people who use mental filters look at everything through black-tinted glasses! They can see only the bad aspects of a situation and are completely blind to the good. For instance, they may list a litany of woes, illnesses, complaints and criticisms but not bother to tell you they've just won Tattslotto!

4. Disqualifying the positive

People who feel they don't deserve to be happy will frequently use this technique to shoot themselves in the foot or make sure they can't feel good. For instance, it's a gloriously sunny morning and you're going on a picnic but they will announce, 'It's sunny now but it's sure to rain later'. They refuse to see positive things in themselves or around them because they feel they are not allowed to be happy or because being miserable brings them secondary payoffs like attention or power.

If you compliment this kind of person they will deny the compliment, denigrate it or point out something negative about themselves instead. This kind of thinking not only makes them gloomy but pulls everyone around them down as well.

5. **Jumping to conclusions**

You can often read other people's body language very accurately. You can be acutely aware of changes in

mood, attitude or feelings in others. However, if you go on to draw conclusions about the reasons behind the mood or behaviour they may be quite inaccurate and unnecessarily self-blaming.

Mind-reading is one form of jumping to conclusions when you assume you know why a person has behaved in a certain way without checking it out. This can lead to awful misunderstandings in relationships.

- A friend fails to return your phone call and you assume the worst – he's not interested in your friendship any more. In fact his answering machine was out of order.

> ✎ *The other kind of jumping to conclusions which can make your life hell is fortune-telling. You are frightened of something happening in the future, but you turn it into a fact even when it hasn't happened!* ✎

- Your wife is evasive and defensive about her Saturday out. You assume she is having an affair when in fact she was shopping for a stereo for your birthday.
- A friend ignores you when you pass in the street. You assume you are being snubbed but then you find out she'd lost a contact lens and didn't see you.

Don't assume – check it out!

The other kind of jumping to conclusions which can make your life hell is fortune-telling. You are frightened of something happening in the future, but you turn it into a fact even when it hasn't happened! In your mind you definitely have Alzheimer's disease, when, like many people at forty, you get a bit absent-minded and forget things.

6. **Magnifying and minimising**

This is the same mental process as using the telescope we talked about earlier to control and manipulate your perspective.

You tend either to make everything worse than it is, 'catastrophising' so that your imperfections become monstrous disabilities, or to shrink anything good about yourself to insignificance.

7. **Emotional reasoning**

This type of thinking causes you to conclude something must be true because you *feel* it is so.

- I *feel* useless ... therefore I *am* useless.
- I *feel* depressed ... therefore I *am* depressed.
- I *feel* inadequate ... therefore I *am* inadequate.
- I *feel* guilty ... therefore I *must be* guilty.

This pattern of 'I *feel*, therefore I *am*' can become a hopeless merry-go-round that is very difficult to jump off unless you recognise that you are using distorted perceptions to trigger bad feelings.

8. **Making lists of 'shoulds' and 'should nots'**

As previously discussed, thinking that is dominated by dogmatic and judgemental lists of what you and others should and should not do will trigger guilt and shame when you fail to meet your own unrealistic demands. You will also become very angry and condemning of others who don't fulfil your expectations of what they should or should not be doing. This kind of thinking promotes hostility, a trait found to be highly correlated with cardiovascular disease.

> *Once you start adopting kinder and more realistic rules for yourself you can stop being so judgemental and condemning of other people.*

Once you start adopting kinder and more realistic rules for yourself you can stop being so judgemental and condemning of other people.

9. **Labelling**

Taking a particular personal mistake and generalising it to a pervasive character trait is an extreme form of generalised thinking. For instance:

- 'I broke a dish, therefore I am a clumsy fool.'
- 'I failed that exam, therefore I'm hopeless at studying.'
- 'My mother was upset because I disagreed with her, therefore I am an ungrateful, insensitive son.'
- 'I burnt the cake, therefore I am a hopeless cook.'

The tendency to do this can be established very early in childhood by parents and teachers attacking a child's whole personality when the child does something wrong:

- 'You're a nuisance, stupid, thick, selfish, ungrateful ...'
- 'You're naughty, bad, impossible, a pain in the neck ...'

If this was done to you, look long and hard at the labels you give yourself and challenge their validity by examining the evidence that conflicts with your label:

- 'I've washed thousands of dishes and only broken one occasionally, therefore I'm not a clumsy fool.'
- 'That's the only exam I've failed in three years, so I'm not a hopeless student.'

- 'I'm allowed to disagree with my mother and we normally have a considerate loving relationship, therefore I'm not an ungrateful, insensitive son.'
- 'I've cooked lots of things without burning them, so I can't be a hopeless cook.'

10. **Personalising**

This involves taking responsibility and blame for things that not only are not your fault but are often none of your business either.

Instead of accepting that you have only a degree of influence over events and people, you take responsibility for controlling everything. In your life, things can't just happen: somebody, inevitably you, has to be blamed and therefore judged and condemned.

> Let others take appropriate responsibility for their actions . . . Unburden yourself, take the hairshirt off and be responsible only for what is really your domain.

If this is you, start to show a little humility. You just don't have that much power! Let others take appropriate responsibility for their actions. Parents who assume responsibility for their children's mistakes (and successes!) have children who grow up believing their parents feel they are incapable of running their own lives. Unburden yourself, take the hairshirt off and be responsible only for what is really your domain. If as a child you were used as the family or class

scapegoat for everything that went wrong, you can now liberate yourself as an adult and give responsibility back to those it really belongs to.

Taking inappropriate responsibility for feelings can be a common trap for women who become the family peacemaker. By stepping in and trying to fix everyone's moods, disagreements and problems, you stop others from realising they have any responsibility for their own feelings, let alone how to develop skills to deal with them.

It's hard to watch your kids in physical and emotional pain, but you insult and undermine them by immediately stepping in, taking control and telling them how to fix things. Teenagers in particular don't want your advice or solutions but instead they want you to listen, to be a sounding-board for them as they explore their *own* solutions. The more you shut up and listen, the more likely they are to actually ask for advice. But even then it is more empowering to suggest possible options for them to consider than to provide a definitive answer.

Teenager: Do you think I should go to the party tonight?

Parent: What are the pros and cons?

Is there anything concerning you about the party?

How could you deal with these concerns?

Can I help in any practical way? (for example, provide a lift home if necessary).

Teenager: Do you think I should do maths next year? I hate it.

Parent: If you dropped maths what would that mean?

If you decide to continue maths is there

any way I could help? (for example, would a tutor be any help?).

This process encourages people to gather more information, explore alternatives and come up with helpful strategies themselves in order to make appropriate decisions.

Even if a decision turns out, with hindsight, to have been unwise, the feeling that it seemed right after proper investigation at the time develops self-confidence.

Feelings

'Rubber band' therapy

To become aware of distorted thinking patterns, you first have to become aware that you are even thinking! To do this, it's often easier to notice what you are feeling and work backwards to the self-talk that caused the feeling. That way, you can modify the self-talk and choose something more constructive. The most effective way to achieve this is through 'rubber band' therapy. Put a firm rubber band on your wrist, and when you become aware of an unwanted feeling pull the rubber band, hard! The pain will freeze the thought or wipe it from your mind completely so that you can now deliberately choose what you want to think and consequently control your feelings.

ROBERT – A CASE STUDY

Robert was 28 and very angry – all the time. His uncontrolled behaviour had caused him to be expelled from two schools as a teenager, and he'd lost count of the jobs from which he'd been sacked for his physical and verbal outbursts. He had three children under five years of age and his wife, although never physically abused by him, had recently left as she was 'sick of being the scapegoat every time he got angry'. Robert had been referred to me by his solicitor because he was now up on charges after deliberately ramming his wife's parked car. Thankfully no one was hurt.

Robert knew a lot about how he felt and had talked endlessly about his feelings to many counsellors. When he stormed into my office for the first time he exclaimed: 'I know how I feel. I've talked about my feelings ad nauseam. But what do I do about them? How do I change them?'

I knew that Robert would never get control of his feelings until he understood that they came mainly from distorted thinking patterns that he was totally unaware of. To get him to slow down his reactions to situations, we used 'rubber band' therapy.

Robert came to realise that his self-talk was extremely self-blaming and self-condemning. Nearly all his anger was directed at himself for never meeting his own expectations: 'I'll never be as successful as my brothers' (he was the second of three boys); 'Mum and Dad don't love me as much because I've caused them so much trouble' (his parents were actually extremely loving and accepting of his difference, which he later admitted); 'I can't do anything right' (although his brothers were academically gifted, Robert was skilled with his hands and demonstrated outstanding survival skills in being able to get work).

'Rubber band' therapy slowed his reactions enough for him to realise what he was thinking, to question its accuracy, and then to replace it with self-talk that was more self-accepting and optimistic. Within a few weeks he was quite overwhelmed by how much happier and in control he felt. A year later he was doing very well in his own business and had successfully reconciled with his wife.

Understanding his self-talk made him confront what he *could* do, not just what he couldn't do. He was then able to create situations in which he could be successful, rather than setting himself up for constant frustration and failure.

Feeling	Self-talk	Alternative self-talk
Guilt	'I shouldn't have said that.'	'It would have been wiser not to have said that but I'm allowed to make mistakes.'
Guilt	'I should've been more patient.'	'Usually I'm patient but I'm allowed to have limits too.'
Guilt	'I shouldn't be so aggressive.'	'I can be needlessly aggressive but I'm trying and I'll change that.'
Uselessness	'I never get anything right.'	'I need to look at why I tend to choose to do things with little chance of success.'
Incompetence	'I'm always the one the boss has to speak to.'	'I don't do this as well as others but then I hate this kind of work. I need work that gives me the chance to do what I know I'm good at.'

'Rubber band' therapy

If nothing changes, nothing changes

Now that you have discovered the connections between thinking and feeling, you have the vital key for unlocking the secrets of happy and healthy people and making them work for you.

Understanding and having the key, however, is not enough. You have to be prepared to use it. That may mean being prepared to look at yourself hard and honestly and then asking yourself to change. If you are reluctant to change, remember that if you always do what you've always done, you'll always get what you've always got!

In short ...

ᘔ You form beliefs based on your perceptions of your experiences.

ᘔ Your beliefs determine your self-talk about yourself and your world. Your feelings come from this self-talk.

ᘔ Knowing and changing your core beliefs enables you to change your self-talk, feelings and reactions to people and situations.

❧ You can adjust your focus so that negative features of your self and your life will blur and fade, and the positive will clearly fill your life screen. Changing your perspective is usually more constructive than trying in vain to change events and other people.

❧ Put your energy into dealing with a situation rather than fighting it.

❧ Modify or get rid of rigid 'should' and 'should not' rules from your thinking.

❧ Be prepared to change.

PART TWO

Secrets of Happy People

The 1st Secret:
Happy people are optimists

Optimism is not simply positive thinking

What is meant by optimism? A common misconception about optimism is that it means always looking for the best in a situation and ignoring the bad: the 'Pollyanna' outlook. As a child I hated that story and Pollyanna in particular. I probably remember my anger and frustration because, like Pollyanna, I had an illness for many months that left me bedridden, in a lot of pain and unable to walk.

> ✍ *A common misconception about optimism is that it means always looking for the best in a situation and ignoring the bad: the 'Pollyanna' outlook.* ✍

To my mind Pollyanna was a dill. My mother, very young, worried sick most of the time and nursing me at home while she ran my father's business, constantly used Pollyanna as an example. I felt more and more wretched, alone and helpless because I didn't feel like Pollyanna. I couldn't ignore my situation and focus on the 'silver lining', another of her favourite phrases at that time. I discovered that if I ignored my mother's attempts to cheer me up I could be quite happy most of the time. I did this by withdrawing more and more into a fantasy world of my own, talking to myself. In my world I was *allowed* to miss my friends, I was *allowed* to feel bored for lack of stimulation. I talked endlessly to my dolls and teddies about how I felt. The telling and silent acceptance and recognition from Teddy, who could not talk back, soon relieved my anguish and so I could become engrossed in some other happy game or endless imagining about what I was going to do when I was better. Once I could talk to Teddy about being sick, I never doubted I would get better.

And I did!

My mother's attempt to focus on the positive rather than on the negative was a well-meaning attempt to stop me from being miserable. However, perhaps due to her own frantic lifestyle, her own fears that I might not get better or might die, or her efforts to try to protect me, it often felt as though she tended to want to deny the reality. This prevented

> ⟍ Whereas positive thinking focuses attention on the outcome of events, optimism focuses on how you explain the causes of these events. ⟍

me from feeling any recognition of what I was going through. Without recognition of my reality I became more and more upset. I felt that even though I *was* sick I wasn't *allowed* to be sick.

So if optimism isn't blind positive thinking, what is it? Whereas positive thinking focuses attention on the outcome of events, optimism focuses on how you explain the causes of these events. Such explanation has three important components: *permanence, pervasiveness* and *personalisation.*

The three faces of optimism

Permanence

People who are optimistic tend to link the good things that happen to them to permanent causes and see the negative events in their lives as having temporary causes. Pessimists do the opposite. Pessimists see good things as having temporary causes and bad events as having permanent causes, especially regarding themselves and their own character traits. For example, in the case of a negative event such as losing a valuable watch:

Pessimist: I'm always losing things.

Optimist: I lost it because I didn't replace the worn strap.

In the case of a positive event such as winning a swimming competition:

Pessimist: It was a fluke, the other competitors were having a bad day.

Optimist: I'm good at swimming.

If you are inclined to use words such as 'always' and 'never' when things go wrong, you are using a self-blaming, pessimistic style of self-talk. But if you can use words like 'sometimes', 'this time', 'recently', then you are seeing negative situations as temporary and therefore changeable in the future. Pessimists condemn the future as well as the present, whereas optimists accurately recognise the present without either condemning or predicting the future. Pessimists see problems in life as similar to falling into a hole. Optimists see such problems as dark patches in a tunnel that has light up ahead and a way out.

If you use a pessimistic style of self-talk, over time you will tend to put in less and less effort and finally you won't even bother trying. But if you use an optimistic style of self-talk and see any success as due to a permanent character trait, you will try even harder the next time, increasing your chances of success even further. The permanent

> ✑ If you want to be happier, start thinking in terms of 'always' rather than 'sometimes' for the good things in life, and 'sometimes' rather than 'always' for the bad! ✑

style of self-talk of optimists extends good things over time, whereas the temporary style of self-talk of pessimists restricts good things to isolated 'flukes' with little chance of their being repeated.

If you want to be happier, start thinking in terms of 'always' rather than 'sometimes' for the good things in life, and 'sometimes' rather than 'always' for the bad!

Pervasiveness

This component of optimism refers to whether you see the causes of events as specific to a particular situation or more universal or global across many situations in life. How pervasively you view causes of events is again revealed by your style of self-talk. For example, if something good happens:

Pessimist *(specific)*:	Optimist *(universal, global)*:
• 'I'm good at football.'	• 'I'm good at sport.'
• 'I got that promotion because I sucked up to the boss.'	• 'I got the promotion because I was the best.'
• 'They only play with me because I own a basketball.'	• 'They play with me because they like me.'

- 'She broke off our engagement because I'm hopeless at relationships.'

- 'She broke off our engagement because we just didn't click.'

The more your self-talk reflects good things happening because of your great general character and bad things happening because of specific situations, the more optimistic you will be. However, it is also important to keep your feet on the ground and not be blinded by optimism that denies realities you should be aware of!

Personalisation

Do you believe causes are internal or external? This component of optimism can be a double-edged sword with pitfalls for both optimists and pessimists. Optimists tend to see other people or external events as being responsible when something goes wrong. Since they don't blame themselves, they feel less guilty and less ashamed than pessimists, who blame themselves for anything and everything going wrong.

Because optimists tend to blame external events, they have higher personal esteem than pessimists, who internalise the blame. But that also means optimists can get very angry when things go wrong, because it's always somebody else's fault!

'If *you* hadn't yelled and upset me this morning when I made a human error and forgot to put out the garbage, I wouldn't have been so distracted that I smashed the car this afternoon!'

The trick is to view what has happened honestly and accurately and take an appropriate degree of individual responsibility for what has occurred. If you are responsible, take the responsibility but see it as a specific temporary lapse (optimistic self-talk), not as a generalised permanent flaw in your character (pessimistic self-talk).

In summary, then:

	Pessimists:	*Optimists:*
Permanence		
• Positive events	Temporary causes	Permanent causes
• Negative events	Permanent causes	Temporary causes
Pervasiveness		
• Positive events	Specific reasons	Global reasons
• Negative events	Global reasons	Specific reasons
Personalisation		
• Positive events	External causes	Internal causes
• Negative events	Internal causes	External causes

Optimism makes you successful

An optimistic style of self-talk has been found to be the single most important predictor of who is successful in life. By success I mean how well you are able to reach your full potential – intellectually, educationally, socially, emotionally and financially – given the limitations of the opportunities available to you, the

traits you inherited and your responsibilities. An optimistic style of self-talk allows you to maximise and seize opportunities when they occur without necessarily compromising your responsibility to others.

(However, do remember that a little pessimism can sometimes allow you to see things more realistically. In life – and especially in business – you may need to temper optimistic thinking with appropriate caution. If you are naturally optimistic and you are dealing with someone who keeps saying 'Yes, but ...', it would be wise to hear them out. Apart from the fact that they may balance your

> ❧ An optimistic style of self-talk has been found to be the single most important predictor of who is successful in life. ❧

enthusiasm with caution, hearing them out shows a respect for and a recognition of their views. It also makes compromise much easier to negotiate!)

Although there does seem to be a significant genetic component to the tendency of a person's style of self-talk, there is also overwhelming evidence that it is influenced by the style of those around you in childhood. There is absolutely no doubt that you can change from a pessimistic to an optimistic style by changing your self-talk and in doing so you can effectively immunise yourself, and your children, from major depression. Doctor Martin Seligman, an American psychologist, recently co-ordinated a Depression Prevention Project for children, with startling results. By teaching children optimistic styles of self-talk, they were able to dramatically decrease the children's chances of developing serious depression. This program is outlined in his book *The Optimistic Child*.

Not only are optimistic people more successful and less likely to become seriously depressed, but they are also healthier, suffer less chronic illness, and make better recovery from serious illness such as cancer or heart disease.

In short ...

- Be a realistic optimist. You don't have to deny real pain. You *are* allowed to feel it.

- Try to avoid using 'permanent' words like 'always' and 'never' when you hit a rough patch. And don't be too ready to blame yourself in your self-talk.

- Terms such as 'this time' or 'sometimes' are better applied to the negative events. This way you give yourself a sporting chance of success the 'next time'.

- Be honest with yourself when things go wrong: it's more likely a temporary lapse (perfectly human) than a permanent character flaw.

- Even if you learnt to look on the black side as a child, it's never too late to unlearn this habit. Change your self-talk to a more optimistic style. The results will astound you.

The 2nd Secret:
Happy people like themselves

The myth that high self-esteem
makes you happy

Happy people have good self-acceptance but not necessarily high self-esteem.

As a newly qualified psychologist working initially as a consultant in schools, I often felt distinctly uneasy about the heavy and increasing emphasis well-meaning teachers and parents placed on making children feel good about themselves regardless of the circumstances. A child's failures, lack of skill or aptitude, and lack of effort were ignored so that only positives were openly discussed. A philosophy emerged that claimed 'everyone is special'; there are no gifted children because everyone is 'gifted'. This led to radical changes in teaching methods and to the complete abandonment of the needs of children with high ability levels (although children with low ability levels were given special attention).

Primary schools were riddled with exercises on 'Who am I?' or 'I am special' that asked children to list all their positive characteristics, usually based on how they compared with other people or how other people saw them: 'I'm pretty' or 'I'm good at running' – ad nauseam.

Although teachers and parents were heavily into the denial that not all children are special (if they are all special then nobody is special by definition), the children themselves were not deluded. Whether you called reading groups red, yellow and blue according to ability, the children still knew that red were best at reading, yellow were average and blue were hopeless. Instead of being allowed to accept their differences, frustrations and inadequacies and then being taught how to deal with them, the children were left in a fantasy land of pretence and denial with no opportunity to learn how to constructively use negative feelings. Failure, with its accompanying frustration, anxiety and challenges, encourages greater effort to achieve mastery and success, but only if the child is not protected from sometimes feeling bad.

'At least you tried' sounds reassuring, but in fact it stifles the expression and explanation of bad and negative feelings. Kids grow up avoiding any situation likely to create bad feelings, because they have had little practice in dealing constructively with such feelings.

A source of great conflict between myself, as a consultant representing the interests of the child and his/her parents, and schools was in deciding whether a child should be promoted to the next grade when it was clear they had not mastered the skills taught in the grade they were in. Teachers were often obsessed with a belief (and a fear) that the discomfort of not going up with their peers would somehow doom them for life. Parents could often see that because of age or for developmental reasons their child needed more time at the same level. Invariably when I spoke to the child there was an enormous sense of wide-eyed relief: 'Could I really stay down?' It was finally being acknowledged that they were struggling, and with sensitive teachers these children benefited enormously from being allowed to move at their own rate.

> ✎ 'At least you tried' sounds reassuring, but in fact it stifles the expression and explanation of bad and negative feelings. ✎

This 'let the child go up regardless of performance' policy is having disastrous consequences at secondary schools. In some state systems a student can enter

Year 7 and decide not to hand in a single piece of work. Unless the parents agree, the school is powerless to keep them down. Consequently you end up with the kids getting the message that no effort is required to proceed through Years 7, 8, 9 and 10. Apart from undermining other students and teachers wanting to take their education seriously, this causes these students to flounder at Year 12 with none of the skills needed to complete their final years of schooling, let alone face the realities of life and the workforce.

High self-acceptance, confidence and self-esteem come from doing things. They come from successfully working around and over obstacles rather than breezing to success with no effort.

Martin Seligman, originator of the depression prevention program, takes this further and hypothesises that one of the reasons we are now having an epidemic of youth suicide is that these child-rearing and teaching practices stop children exploring and using negative feelings constructively. From my own clinical experience I have to say I tend to agree that this could be one of the vital factors in the complex causes of an increase in youth suicide.

> ☙ High self-acceptance, confidence and self-esteem come from doing things. They come from successfully working around and over obstacles rather than breezing to success with no effort. ☙

High self-esteem based on *external* measures of your worth and how you compare with others actually makes you emotionally very vulnerable. If for some reason you can no longer be a great footballer or are retrenched from your job, you no longer have this externally given self-worth. So what's left? Who are you without your job, your membership of a club, your sport, your public positions?

A group of doctors I was giving a lecture to on this topic became extremely defensive at this suggestion. They could not accept that so much of their self-worth was driven by their profession – until I asked them to think about who they were without their stethoscopes. The shocked and uncomfortable silence that followed clearly demonstrated how hollow their self-esteem was.

If your self-opinion and self-esteem are based on labels (see page 56), you are even more vulnerable. Labels have inherent value judgements attached to them. They are often negative and illogical, incorporating generalised opinions that are often personal attacks on you: clumsy, idiot, silly, hopeless, useless, bitch, dill, stupid, dumb, nerd, wimp, scatterbrain, airhead ... Even positive labels have value judgements attached to them comparing you, or your achievements, with others: pretty, clever, intelligent, caring, conscientious ... If the labels are given to you by others you feel good, but if you depend on them for your self-worth then you have to live with the fact that others may take away or change that label if you don't continually live up to it. This keeps you insecure, anxious and a victim of other people's values.

Avoiding the trap of feeling good because of external opinions of you and your achievements means avoiding labels and sticking to the facts. Facts concentrate only on what you did, not on who you are. They are specific rather than global, so even if you've made a monstrous mistake only the mistake is attacked, not you as a person. For example, 'I lost today, but I'm not a loser. This is not the end of my life' (Greg Norman on losing the 1996 US Masters Golf Tournament).

If others try to label you, use your internal self-talk to change the label into a specific action. For example:

External label: You're stupid, you smashed the car.

Internal self-talk: I smashed the car and he's upset.

External label: You're a pain in the neck.

Internal self-talk: I'm annoying him at the moment and he wants to be alone.

If you are dealing with other people, you can promote self-acceptance and self-liking in them by always sticking to the facts and never using labels. People who like themselves are much easier to deal with, so it's in your interest to promote happiness not only in yourself but also in others.

If you constantly rate your worth as a person on an external barometer, you tend to worry a great deal about what others think. To protect yourself from being scrutinised too carefully you put up barriers both to realistic self-appraisal and to the appraisal of others. The fear of not being thought well of by

others makes you avoid risks and new situations and makes it difficult, if not impossible, to take appropriate blame or responsibility if something goes wrong: 'They might discover the idiot I really am'. You can become totally controlled by trying to please others to gain positive feedback about your worth. Alternatively you're so consumed by your own worries that you become self-centred.

If you constantly rate your worth as a person on an external barometer, you tend to worry a great deal about what others think.

In relationships, relying on an external barometer of your worth can make it impossible for you to work collaboratively because you must win, you must be better — not just different. You tend to see people as either on your side or actively against you. You see ambivalence in others as a judgement against you. Your self becomes like an air-filled sponge; bland, with no substance. It is only attractive when you add external extras on top: icing, sprinkles, lollies, cream, chocolates. It's the extras that make it taste good.

But when you start to accept yourself, you are like a luscious fruitcake, with a rich full-flavoured body and firm texture, spiked with glistening jewels of fruit and nuts. Any decorations placed on top are a bonus, but the cake itself is richly fulfilling and can stand alone.

Self-acceptance makes you happier

Self-acceptance allows you to be comfortable with all aspects of yourself, good and bad. You feel confident that you can change if you want to change. You can be yourself; you don't need to hide behind a role. Because you are not competing with others, you can work collaboratively to fix a mistake or to solve a problem. You can accept other people's mistakes and you can genuinely enjoy their successes, because their mistakes and their successes make no difference to your own sense of self-worth. Accepting yourself frees you to make rules and to change rules according to your own needs and responsibilities, not other people's.

> ☜ *Self-acceptance allows you to be comfortable with all aspects of yourself, good and bad.* ☜

The freedom to choose your own rules liberates you from unnecessary guilt. Once you no longer keep rating the worth of yourself and others, you can enjoy the challenge of competition and winning without needing to reaffirm yourself. Accepting yourself allows you to enjoy the doing rather than focusing on the outcome. It becomes easier to live in the moment and therefore to be happier.

JADE – A CASE STUDY

Jade was fifteen and a brilliant, gifted athlete. Ever since she was at primary school she had excelled at running. She ran because she just loved the feeling of the air moving against her body. She'd run in the sun or in the rain. The light track clothing made her feel free and relaxed as she moved.

But then she was chosen for serious training as a potential Olympian. The focus was no longer on the joy of running but on goals, trophies and medals. The coaches were beside themselves with her ability and soon Jade's parents also became consumed with the goal of winning. Jade had always liked to win but for her it had been a bonus, the icing on the cake. It was the actual running that gave her joy.

Jade had always enjoyed the approval of others but had never really needed it. Within twelve months of serious training she was severely depressed and literally running out of control. It was only when she refused point-blank to move to the blocks at the start of a championship that her coaches and parents started to listen.

Do you *need* approval or do you simply *enjoy* approval?

If your self-worth is externally based, you will be constantly pursuing approval and adjusting your life to gain it from others. But if you truly accept yourself you will enjoy approval as an incidental bonus, while being motivated in your life by what gives you satisfaction and pleasure.

This does not mean that you become oblivious to other people's opinions or needs, or your responsibilities to others. We are social animals that must naturally support each other. Self-acceptance and self-liking mean you are appropriately aware of your responsibilities to others and of what is an appro-

> *Accepting yourself makes it easier to accept the blemishes and failures of others without judgement and condemnation.*

priate degree of influence for them on you and for you on them. But accepting yourself makes it easier to accept the blemishes and failures of others without judgement and condemnation. Eliminating hostility promotes better interpersonal relationships generally.

Being yourself

One of the most rewarding aspects of liking and accepting yourself is the relief of being able to be yourself. There's no need to hide behind a role or image, no need to build a fort around yourself so others can't see the terrible *real* you.

Liking and being yourself also protects your sense

of self from external changes in your life. When you are *you*, regardless of your job, friends, interests and achievements, you are more resilient and able to adapt with yourself intact if these things are threatened. If your identity is not dependent on any one particular aspect of yourself, be it a job or a skill, you will have tremendous freedom to experiment with lots of other activities and occupations: you can focus on enjoying the doing, which is what happiness is all about.

> ✎ *Many people don't allow themselves to be themselves. Instead they squash themselves into moulds of other people's expectations.* ✎

Many people don't allow themselves to be themselves. Instead they squash themselves into moulds of other people's expectations: their parents', friends', spouse's or peers'.

TONY AND BILL – TWO CASE STUDIES

Tony had always loved working with wood. His parents were both professionals who thought Tony's extraordinary skills were fine as a hobby but certainly not to be considered for a future occupation. He attended highly academic schools where his reports repeatedly said Tony was not working to his ability. He knew himself that his 'A's could have been 'A⁺'s but he hated the academic subjects and preferred art, graphics and technology. He fulfilled the school's and his parents' expectations anyway and studied computer science.

In his late twenties Tony came to see me, seriously depressed. His work paid him handsomely and gave him and his wife an enviable lifestyle. But as we explored what made him happy, it became obvious that Tony's need for an active physical lifestyle and an outlet for the extraordinary creativity that bubbled in his mind were being constantly stifled.

Unfortunately Tony's wife could not accept the idea of being married to a carpenter rather than a computer programmer, and after months of anguish and his being on antidepressant medication, they separated.

A year later he wrote to me about his wonderful new life and described feeling as if he had been released after years in prison. The depression was long gone and he was now doing all kinds of highly skilled woodwork, had a new relationship and didn't mind the huge drop in income.

'I now feel like I'm *me* and my parents are just going to have to get used to the idea that their son is not what *they* want him to be.'

Bill was twenty-four and was referred to me by his psychiatrist and physician. Two years previously his father had developed emphysema and his health was deteriorating rapidly. Bill hated school and had left at the age of fourteen. He had worked, or more accurately had slaved, on his parents' large dairy farm ever since. He had no social life, and soon after his father's illness was diagnosed he developed severe asthma, which stopped him from working. Both parents had expected Bill to take over the farm 'one day' but in the meantime he had been paid little and desperately wanted to become a chef and work with people. Bill's highly extroverted and likeable personality was totally at odds with life on this isolated farm.

He soon realised that the physician and psychiatrist had been right and that his sudden asthma attack was more psychological than physical. He was unable to separate himself from his father's expectations to the point where he took on his father's health problems as well.

Finally his parents were forced to sell the farm and Bill no longer felt obliged to live with them. He took a job, first as a kitchen hand and then as an adult apprentice. By the time he graduated from college as a chef his asthma had disappeared.

If you feel a sense of pervasive unhappiness and discontent with your life, it may be worth exploring why you are doing the things you do. We all have responsibilities to others but this must be balanced by considering your responsibility to yourself.

So often I see young people struggling with higher education or particular courses because everyone tells them education is crucial to their future. But languishing in a course or lifestyle you hate can stop you discovering your real talents in the workforce. Some young people need to try working before they can really discover what they are good at and what they would actually enjoy studying.

In short ...

- It's better to acknowledge and to learn to deal with your less charming characteristics and inadequacies than to live in a fantasy land of never feeling bad.

- Learn to explore and use your negative feelings constructively.

- Don't look only to external measures of your self-worth. This can make you vulnerable if or when these externals fail you.

- Don't hang value-laden labels on yourself – either negative or positive. They are probably based on other people's value systems anyway.

- Don't be controlled by a desire to please others in order to boost your self-worth.

❧ Enjoy the relief of liking and accepting yourself. You'll be free to enjoy the doing, you won't be intimidated by the outcome and you'll be able to live in the moment. This is being really happy.

❧ Consider your responsibility to yourself as well as to others.

The 3rd Secret: Happy people have a sense of personal control

Who's in control?

One of the strongest predictors of who feels happy is the degree to which an individual feels in personal control of their life.

If you tend to think 'the average person can influence government decisions', you would have a strong internal locus of control. However, if you think 'the world is run by a few powerful people' then you would have an external locus of control.

A sense of control over your life also improves your health. An experiment done in a nursing home gave each patient on one floor a pot plant to look after. Patients on another floor were given pot plants that the staff looked after. Those patients looking after the pot plants were also given a choice of meals whereas the other patients were given the same meals but on days determined by the staff. At the end of one year 93 per cent of those patients who had been given more control of their daily lives were more alert and active, happier and healthier than the patients given no more control.

Animals put in a highly stressful situation that they could not control had tumours that grew much more rapidly than the

> ⟆ A sense of control over your life improves your health. ⟆

tumours in animals that could control the stress of the situation (in this case being able to stop electric shocks).

In the workplace, giving workers more control over their work space, air temperature and decision-making has consistently improved productivity and the level of job satisfaction, and has decreased sick leave.

JIM AND HELEN – A CASE STUDY

Jim and Helen both held good jobs, which should have given them and their three children relative security and a high standard of living. Helen had been educated at an exclusive girls' boarding school and Jim had been educated in the State system. Helen had enjoyed and appreciated her own privileged education, which had given her many advantages. Jim felt he had missed out and was determined his children would be educated at the best private schools.

When the children entered secondary school, fees and extras began eating up all Helen's income and some of Jim's as well. Within the prevailing economic climate, the future of both their jobs became uncertain and they lived in constant fear that they might have to withdraw their children from their schools.

This fear came to dominate their lives and great tension developed in their relationship. Jim worked harder and harder, taking every promotion he could get to try to accumulate a reserve of funds in case one of them lost their job.

Neither did, but Jim developed serious heart disease. He was faced with a choice: either reduce his working hours or lose his life. When he came to see me he was contemplating suicide, as he rationalised that the insurance would allow his children to finish their private education!

Most distressing for Jim and Helen was the feeling that their lives were not theirs to live but were controlled by some external factor: school fees. It was Jim's children who eventually straightened out his thinking. They told him how much they had missed him when he went overseas on regular business trips and that although changing schools would be hard, losing their dad would be infinitely worse.

Consequently, Jim took a less demanding job in the same company and the family moved to a smaller but more expensive house in order to be in the zoning for a highly regarded State secondary school. Suddenly the family had money for the theatre, good holidays and leisure activities, as well as more relaxed time together as a family. Jim's health improved dramatically and he described his enjoyment and happiness as being greater than at any time in his life.

Reassessing their priorities and values had been difficult for Jim and Helen. They had locked themselves into thinking 'our children should go to private schools', and it was hard to change. They also had to challenge the rules in their heads that said 'Children won't receive their best chance in life at a State school' and 'Parents are totally responsible for their children's chances at success'. However, once they accepted the realities of their financial situation they were able to find a constructive alternative.

Jim and Helen came to realise that their old assumptions implied that their children had little control or input into their own education: the parents unwittingly fostered a belief that their children's futures were solely determined by the particular schools they attended.

To have an internal locus of control does not mean thinking you are in absolute and total control of (and therefore to blame for) everything that happens to you. It does not mean believing 'I chose to be molested as a child' or 'I choose to be sick'. These kinds of beliefs are attractive to some people because they deny the reality that they can't actually control everything that happens.

Having an internal locus of control means that you tend to see yourself as having an influence over your life. You don't see yourself as a helpless victim buffeted every which way by life.

You determine how stressed you feel

In order to have a sense of personal control, you need to have a very good understanding of the chain reaction linking events, thoughts and feelings.

It is not the events themselves that are inherently stressful but the meaning we attach to these events. Some years ago I worked with groups of army wives who were constantly moving as their husbands were reposted. Most of these women had had to move several times in the previous two years, and they and their children were severely affected by the constant breaking of friendships and changes of school.

However, as each woman related her tale of misery (quite justified I thought) one woman said nothing. After an hour of anguished weeping by the others in the group, this woman suddenly said, 'Well, I don't

understand you all. Moving all the time is great. I don't have to put up with the same decor, the army paints the house I'm moving into, I make new friends and my kids have pen pals all over the Pacific. Every holiday we go and stay with a different old friend at one of the previous postings. It's marvellous'.

We all gaped at this woman's happiness with her situation. The same situation (and she had actually moved the most in the shortest time) had a totally different

> It is not events themselves that are inherently stressful but the meaning we attach to events.

meaning for her. But what was particularly interesting was the effect she had on the other women. By then, they had all had their chance to fully express their anguish and have it recognised, so her comments helped them to steer their own thinking in quite a different direction. Within a short time there was much laughter and hope as they swapped funny stories about people and places, removalists, lost belongings and children's reactions, and started to actually plan and look at their next move quite differently.

These women had suddenly discovered that they had a choice about how they perceived the situation and what beliefs they developed about it. Their self-talk changed and consequently so did their feelings. They realised that if they pooled their experiences they could write a short survival manual for moving and making new friends — for themselves and for their children at their new schools. Sharing and learning these moving skills dramatically reduced the stress of the next move: they had the necessary skills to deal with the situation, and they had more control.

It's your choice

When you are faced with the responsibility for something you don't want to do but feel you should, it can relieve the anguish considerably to say to yourself 'I don't have to do this, but I choose to'.

When my grandmother was in a nursing home for some years, visiting her could be an emotionally draining and depressing occasion. I felt for her having to live there and knew that taking her young great-grandchildren to visit was something she really enjoyed. Once I started to say to myself 'I *choose* to visit her' rather than 'I *have* to visit her', my feelings also changed. I actually found it quite easy and pleasant to think of things to do with her and with the children whenever we visited.

> Saying 'I choose ...' puts the locus of control back inside you, whereas saying 'I have to ...' externalises the control. It makes you feel a victim of circumstances and of other people's demands.

Nobody is holding a gun to your head, so saying 'I choose ...' puts the locus of control back inside you, whereas saying 'I have to ...' externalises the control. It makes you feel a victim of circumstances and of other people's demands.

Controlling time

Happy people also take control of their time. They make manageable plans and commitments. They are busy, purposeful and punctual. Activity promotes happy feelings whereas aimlessness, boredom, and poor time management is a characteristic of unhappy people.

> ✎ If you want to be happy, you need to act happy and that means doing the things that happy people do. ✎

If you want to be happy, you need to act happy and that means doing the things that happy people do. It is a myth to think that you can't do more or do happy things until you *are* happy. Happiness is very much a state in which the pleasant things in life outnumber the unpleasant, and in which there are high experiences of intense pleasure to look forward to, for example a weekend away or seeing a show.

Sorting out your priorities

To have time for the pleasant things in life you may have to become ruthless about your priorities. There just isn't enough time in the day or money in the bank to do everything. To stop feeling overwhelmed and to give yourself more time, simplify your life. Consider the following:

• How much of what you do is necessary, how much

is habit and how much is 'because everybody else is doing it'?

- Which relationships are important to you, which are no longer relevant and which are 'dead'?

- What do you really need in your home and what is unnecessary clutter? (If you haven't used, appreciated or worn something in the last twelve months, maybe it's time to get rid of it. The fewer possessions you have the less time you have to spend looking after them.) How big a house and mortgage do you really need?

- What do you *need* and what do you *want*? (Sort out your financial priorities in this way. Get good financial advice, budget, and liberate yourself from future debt by cutting up your credit cards.)

Simplifying your life by reducing it to basic needs and to necessary and rewarding commitments gives you more time, money and energy for yourself and your *real* responsibilities. When you start sorting out your priorities, you start controlling your life.

You *can* stop worrying

You may believe it is impossible for you to feel a sense of personal control because you can't stop worrying. Worrying keeps you focused on the past and the future, which makes it impossible to enjoy the present.

To stop worrying you can:

Try 'rubber band' therapy (see page 60).   This is a way of stopping unwanted intrusive thoughts. The sharp pain wipes the thought and allows you to choose to focus on something more pleasant.

Practise self-talk.   A very powerful form of self-talk for constant worriers is to say to yourself, 'No matter what happens, I know I can somehow cope with whatever I have to'. At the same time take a deep breath and breathe out slowly, imagining all tension draining away as your body fills with new energy.

It is very important to remember that as a human being you have been designed to cope with a great many unhappy and sad things – 'the roughage of life' – as well as the good things in life. Even terminal illness can be coped with extremely well if you allow yourself to cope and make use of any outside help you may need. *Many things happen that we don't want to happen, but that doesn't mean that we can't deal with them.*

When I was being threatened and harassed on the

phone by people unhappy with my last book, I had to stop and say to myself, every time the phone rang, 'No matter what this call is about I can stay calm and comfortable and deal with it in the most appropriate way'.

I surprised even myself at how well I could manage difficult and dangerous situations with this self-talk.

Set aside 'worry time'.   Another useful strategy is to set aside a 'worry time' each day so that the rest of the time you can focus on the 'now', not on the future or the past.

As something that's worrying you comes to mind, write it down and deal with it later in your worrying session. Make the duration of your worrying session the same each day, perhaps fifteen minutes. Allow yourself to relax and contemplate each concern. Explore possible solutions. Break down each concern into the things you can and can't do about it.

Make time for exercise.   For distress that causes physical pain, particularly in your chest, aerobic exercise or using weights to work the upper body may be the only way to get relief. (But first make sure the pains in your chest are emotional, not physical.) Very distressing situations create stress hormones that build up, particularly in the cardiovascular system, increasing the deposition of plaque in blood vessels. Sweating from hard exercise is a highly effective way of releasing these hormones from the body. Even better is exercise that involves social contact such as dancing, gym work or team sports, because it helps distract you from your troubles.

Allow yourself to enjoy this moment.   Patients find that one of the most difficult things to cope with is waiting for medical test results with a possible life-threatening outcome. For many the uncertainty of not knowing what they are facing can be more difficult when a series of tests are taken over months or years of check-ups to monitor the progress of a previously treated illness such as cancer.

You can start to feel that your whole life revolves around these tests, that your life is suspended as you approach a test and then wait for the results. Coping with this situation entails focusing very much on each second. Ask yourself if you are prepared to allow yourself to really enjoy this moment; to ignore the past and the future. Focus instead on fully experiencing each moment as it occurs.

> *Focus on fully experiencing each moment as it occurs.*

Turn anxiety into specific fears.   For those facing greater and greater dependence on others as illness progresses, the need to do what you can do and accept what you can't becomes even more important. If you feel anxiety as a generalised sensation, turn it into a specific fear and do what you can about that. If you have disturbing physical symptoms or are recovering from serious illness or trauma, don't worry about unexplained symptoms: do something about them. Ring your doctor or have tests. Find out specifically what you are dealing with. Imagine the relief if you find your fears are groundless, and reassure yourself that even if the news is not welcome, you will be able to find the resources you need to deal with it.

If you are frightened of dying, work out exactly what bothers you about death. Is it the process of dying that worries you? Are you concerned about what will happen to your family? Do you have religious concerns? Are you bothered by the thought of your spouse marrying someone else? Get help to deal with the practical aspect of your fears; good counselling will help you with the spiritual or emotional aspects.

If you worry about your teenage children, think about what specifically you are frightened of: unprotected sex? drunk driving? sexually transmitted diseases? drugs? dubious friendships? all of the above?! By focusing on your specific fear you can deal precisely with that subject by providing

> Whatever the fear, don't just think about it: do something about it!

information, transport, or effective listening. If all of the above are a problem, maybe you need to seek some expert help in dealing with the situation. Whatever the fear, don't just think about it: do something about it!

Make decisions.　Worriers often have great difficulty making decisions because they are frightened of the consequences of being wrong.

If this is you, remind yourself that decisions can be made only based on the information available at the time. On weighing the pros and cons, make a decision and allow yourself the right to perhaps be wrong in hindsight. Remind yourself that nobody makes decisions without sometimes making mistakes. It's often better to make a wrong decision than to make no decision at all. Tell yourself 'I'm allowed to make a mistake' and 'I know that no matter what the outcome I'll be able to find the resources to deal with the consequences'.

Take time-out.　Sometimes worrying develops because you really need a holiday or some time-out from the routine and hassle of everyday life. Worrying about little things can mean that you need to take a break either for a few minutes or a whole day or a few weeks. It can be the first sign of a general burn-out, so treat it seriously.

Occasionally all you need to do is to continue living your usual life, but begin to ruthlessly discard what isn't strictly your business. 'See no evil, hear no evil, speak no evil' for a while. Avoid all bad news on

TV, radio and newspapers until you feel you are able to keep a better sense of proportion.

When worrying becomes obsession

It is perfectly normal to worry, even to worry a lot. However, if you find yourself preoccupied not only by thoughts but also by images or impulses, or if you feel compelled to carry out some ritual to try to neutralise anxiety, you may have an obsessive compulsive condition. Once properly diagnosed, these conditions can be treated extremely well. If you suspect this is you, consult a psychologist trained to treat obsessions and compulsions with a treatment called cognitive behaviour therapy. Often this condition is associated with clinical depression that may not be obvious. It is essential that the depression is also treated.

> ℞ It is perfectly normal to worry, even to worry a lot. ℞

Whose responsibility is it?

To have a sense of personal control also means taking only appropriate responsibility for your own and other people's feelings and/or behaviour. Some people tend to try to make other people feel better, becoming family peacemakers burdened by other people's problems. Others tend to try to control behaviour, either their children's or their spouse's.

It's often difficult enough in life managing your own feelings and actions without loading yourself up with other people's. Some of us use controlling others as a way of escaping our own conflicts, unsatisfying relationships or difficult behaviour, saying to ourselves 'If only you were happier, nicer, kinder ..., then I would be happy'.

Teenagers commonly use their parents as scapegoats for everything wrong in their lives: 'They don't understand me'.

It can be quite healthy for teenagers to start to have a more realistic picture of their parents' strengths and weaknesses in order to become more independent and develop their own sense of self. But this does not have to be a destructive condemnation of their parents' bewildered attempts to muddle through parenthood, often with only very poor parenting role models in their own background.

If teenagers start to take more responsibility for their own feelings and actions and stop blaming everyone else, they are not only empowering and making themselves happier, but they also allow a far deeper and more adult-to-adult relationship to develop with their parents.

Taking responsibility for others' problems

Abdicating responsibility for yourself or poking your nose into other people's business will have two destructive consequences.

Firstly, people resent your interference and get irritable and angry with you. They get angry because you are giving them clear messages that you don't think they are capable of solving their own problems. The more you control your children's lives physically and emotionally, the more dependent and less secure they will become. This is not to say you abandon them, but rather from a very early age you encourage them to do as much for themselves as possible — physically and emotionally. Children and adults need loving support, but they don't generally need you to give them all the answers and to fix the problem.

For instance, if your child complains of being teased you could march down to the school next morning, child in tow, and demand that everyone from the principal down 'do something about it'! Or you could empathise with how hurt your child feels and help them explore what is also going on in their own head about the teasing.

> The more you control your children's lives physically and emotionally, the more dependent and less secure they will become.

Help them identify their own self-talk. 'He said

I'm dumb, therefore I am dumb, so I feel stupid.'

Help them to realise that someone else's label isn't necessarily true and that they can change the voice in their head to 'He said I'm dumb, but what would he know? I can find maths tricky but I can read well and tell great stories and ... so I'm definitely not dumb'.

Even very young children are impressed to realise that they can control their feelings by the self-talk in their heads. Of course, if the teasing is not a minor isolated incident then you should notify the school immediately.

When someone starts to tell you their problems, just listen instead of coming up with all the answers, or if asked for advice, explore different options but insist they decide the best option for themselves.

The more you either state or give the impression that you believe they have the ability to choose the best option for themselves, the more they tend to live up to that trust and faith.

The second thing that happens when you take responsibility away from others is that you end up worn out. If you go around trying not to upset anyone, you inevitably put your own needs last and nobody ever listens to *your* problems. They suck you dry and move

> ✒ It can be a wonderful relief to hand back the problem to the person it belongs to. ✒

on, leaving you gasping. It can be a wonderful relief to hand back the problem to the person it belongs to:

- 'Where is my maths book?'
  'I don't know, go and look for it.'
- 'I haven't got any socks.'
  'The drawer was full of socks. Look harder.'
- 'He won't turn the music down.'
  'Perhaps you had better talk to him.'
- 'That daughter of yours is getting very cheeky.'
  'Perhaps you had better talk to her.'
- 'Johnny is upset about his exams; you can get through to him better than I can.'
  'In that case you had better talk to him so you can practise how to get through to him.'
- 'If you hadn't insisted I do my chores I wouldn't have been late for football practice.'
  'If you had taken responsibility for doing your chores instead of watching TV you wouldn't have been late.'

Before you blindly step in to solve either an emotional upset or a problem, STOP and ask yourself two questions:

- 'Whose problem is this?'
- 'Whose responsibility is this?'

Only then take appropriate responsibility, if any, for fixing it. Put the responsibility back where it should be and insist that those responsible solve it. Initially people will be annoyed with you as they are used to using you and not having to learn the skills to do what's necessary themselves. But once they get the message they will start to enjoy the responsibility because it empowers them with more personal control of their own lives.

That's one of the secrets of being happy.

In business this can mean not just happier workers but much more profitable businesses. A manager needs to learn to direct responsibility and facilitate an environment where possible solutions are offered for his or her consideration rather than allowing problems to be dumped on his or her desk. The more managers are able to put faith in those directly responsible for creating the solutions, the more personal control these workers will feel and therefore the greater the personal satisfaction they will have in what they are doing.

> ❧ The energy gained from no longer carrying the world's problems makes you feel lighter, bouncier and happier. ❧

The energy gained from no longer carrying the world's problems makes you feel lighter, bouncier and happier.

Personal boundaries

Many people would love to off-load all that inappropriate responsibility but they find it hard to work out how much or how little responsibility they should feel. Either they build a wall around themselves and don't let anyone in, or they are unable to create appropriate personal space.

This is particularly the case with anyone who has grown up in an abusive environment where their physical, emotional or sexual space has been violated or not allowed to develop.

One of the most insidious consequences of child abuse is that the child, then the adult they become, does not feel they have any right to a personal private space. They come to believe that anyone can intrude right to the centre of their being and, depending on the abuse, this can be the emotional, physical or sexual self. In fact there is little concept of self; they belong to others, who do with them what they wish.

This can also happen with people who have never been abused but who are particularly emotionally sensitive and have never been encouraged or allowed to develop limits to their sensitivity for their own survival. Sensitive people can be easy to manipulate for the benefit of others. The child who senses friction between his or her parents and so does everything to

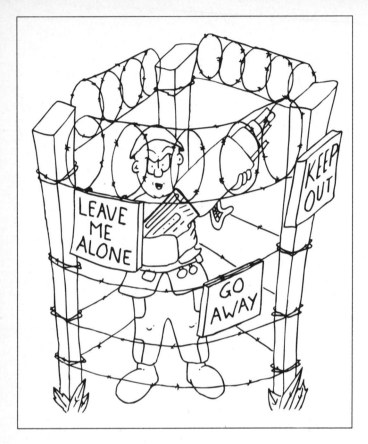

keep the peace between them can be unconsciously or quite deliberately used by the parents as the peacemaker, not only in the parental relationship but in sibling relationships as well.

The following diagram illustrates the concept of appropriate personal boundaries. A young baby does not see itself as separate from its mother. The baby becomes distressed when its mother is away or out of

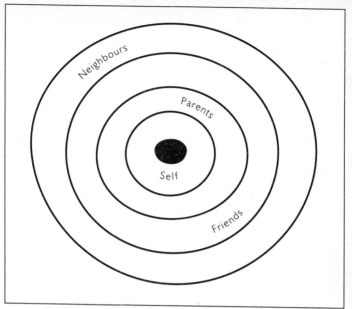

Appropriate personal boundaries

sight because the degree of closeness is such that their personal boundaries are tightly intertwined. As the baby grows, and plays with its toes to explore its own physical boundaries, it also begins to explore its world. With development comes a stronger and stronger sense of self as separate from others and the environment. If the growth of this self-concept is allowed and nurtured, the child develops independence and self-confidence. In the teenage years healthy development means that the concept of self becomes even stronger and the relative emotional position and distance of family and friends starts to change.

The strong centre spot in the diagram represents you. Each concentric circle surrounding this spot is an emotional boundary. With healthy emotional development your family, friends and acquaintances will be at different distances from you, so some people will be allowed closer to you than others, and some people will be allowed to influence you more than others. The important thing is that it is up to you to decide and control which people are within which boundaries. In this way you will not be overwhelmed by competing and conflicting demands. Demands and influences will be prioritised according to what suits you and will vary at different times in your life. When you are a child your parents may be in the innermost ring, but when you are an adult your spouse or children may occupy this space and your parents assume a more distant space.

If you feel overwhelmed by emotional and physical demands from other people, it can be useful to draw this diagram, placing people at different distances from yourself so that you prioritise your relationships. This makes it much easier to take only appropriate responsibility for issues. It is still necessary to recognise even those closest to you as separate from yourself. When you meet someone, immediately place them on an appropriate boundary (this can change later). In this way you can control the level of your involvement with different people. Claim your personal space so that you are not owned by others.

Those of you who are very sensitive or who have been abused may need to first establish yourself as having the right to have a personal space: physically, emotionally and sexually. People in these categories often have no real personal boundaries at all and everything that happens to everyone else is felt as if it is happening to them as well. They suffer with the people in war zones; they suffer with their neighbour's cancer; they feel the anguish of the death of a local child whom they don't even know; a bird killed by a car and dead on the road pains them; their children's rejection or failure at school tortures them; their sibling's marriage difficulty haunts them; their husband's lack of confidence distresses them. These people have no filters. Every bit of conflict, anguish, unhappiness or pain in the world is like an arrow shooting towards them and piercing their heart. It's very common for them to live, literally, with constant heartache and an aching jaw.

> ᘾ Once you allow yourself to claim your right to a self with personal space, and you place the people in your life within different boundaries, you suddenly take control. ᘾ

Such a lack of filters and boundaries around

Claim your right to a personal space

yourself means that you have little sense of personal control and feel a victim of an unhappy and anguished world. It is common to end up in abusive family or work situations as you continue to allow people to dump their rubbish onto you. However, once you allow yourself to claim your right to a self with personal space, and you place the people in your life within different boundaries, you suddenly take control. The boundaries become see-through shields like bullet-proof glass allowing you to see and hear what's going on, but controlling how far you allow things into your space, if at all. In this way you can imagine yourself observing lots of things but deliberately choosing your degree of involvement and type of response.

Developing a clear idea of your personal space and your personal boundaries allows you to recognise more clearly what is an appropriate degree of responsibility, and also what your priorities are.

Priorities can be cultural dynamite, because what are accepted priorities in one culture can be totally unacceptable in another ...

When an Australian Prime Minister cancelled an offical visit to Japan to be with his wife while she had major surgery, the Australian community was completely supportive that he put his family needs and responsibilities first. However, Japan was outraged. In Japanese society public duty comes before family and many sections of the Japanese community saw his actions as an insult to Japan.

Cultures and people who do put family needs above duty to country or employer report much higher levels of happiness than those where there is continual personal sacrifice to the needs (as stated by the government) of the country or an employer.

Creating and controlling appropriate personal boundaries does not mean abdicating proper responsibility to and for others. As you will read later, feeling socially and emotionally connected, committed and responsible to and for other people is vital for happiness and for physical and emotional health.

The key is balance, and the crucial word is *appropriate*. A healthy degree of self-centredness allows you to create appropriate boundaries so that you don't walk around suffering everybody else's pain and trying to solve everybody else's problems. On the other hand, selfishness stops you from being able to empathise with other people. If you can't empathise, it is almost impossible to form harmonious communities and long-term, healthy relationships between individuals.

The often cruel selfishness now being promoted and applauded by politicians under the euphemism of 'individualism' is the antithesis of what is needed to make us healthier and happier — as individuals and as communities. Policies that reduce individuals' responsibilities to each other lead to personal and social distress and deep insecurity. Not only does the health and happiness of individuals suffer, but the fears generated can lead to divisive intolerance and violence.

If we want happy and safe communities, the message to corporations and governments is clear: to foster *long-term*, productive and peaceful communities, human needs — based on appropriate, shared responsibility — must take priority.

Standing up for yourself

Once you can recognise how much responsibility you should take about an issue it can be quite another matter to stand up for yourself.

Personal interactions tend to fall into three main styles:

- assertive
- passive
- aggressive.

From my professional experience most of us grow up in families that operate in either a passive or an aggressive manner towards each other. If your preferred style is passive, you may also be highly manipulative in order to get your own way. You don't know how to do things directly, so you do it indirectly.

Aggressive and passive styles are closely allied to the physiological fight-or-flight responses that we experience when threatened. When angered or cornered by a threat, the tendency is to run away. If we can't run away, we try to make ourselves invisible so that we won't continue to be attacked. Alternatively, we may be forced to become aggressive to defend ourselves. The fight-or-flight physiological response is not

> ◊ *Aggressive and passive styles are closely allied to the physiological fight-or-flight responses that we experience when threatened.* ◊

confined to physical threats; it is generated by emotional threats as well.

In relationships and human interactions, the start of potential problems is the start of the chain mentioned on page 16: the perceptions that each person has of a particular event or interchange. If each person or at least one person hasn't learnt to manage and control the accuracy and appropriateness of their perceptions, beliefs, self-talk, feelings and responses in the chain reaction, then ordinary interactions can be fraught with misunderstandings and misrepresentations that are perceived as threats. Depending on the style of response (aggressive or passive) that you have seen in your own role models and your personality, you will tend to respond either passively or aggressively.

An aggressive person respects their rights and gives no rights or respect to the other person. If you are aggressive, perhaps you need to remember that you don't have to be very clever to get your own way. To treat others with respect and to be unselfish takes integrity, honesty and an honourable personal moral code.

A passive person acknowledges and respects the needs and rights of others but puts their own needs and rights last.

Standing up to an aggressive person is particularly

difficult if they have or take more power, and are physically bigger than you and use their size to intimidate or bully you by invading your personal space. Although the assertive option is usually the best option to try, there are many situations where being passive is safer or where aggression is warranted for your own defence and safety.

For instance, if you are mugged by someone who is armed, definitely take the passive stance. If a policeman pulls you over on the road, be passive. If your physical safety is threatened, depending on your assessment of the relative power of each person, you may decide to be passive or aggressive, but rarely assertive.

Yet there are some people who are used to using aggressive tone, body language, volume and physical presence to get their own way. Under these circumstances you may well find you simply have to raise your own voice, tone and so on simply to be heard, but you can still keep your words assertive rather than aggressive. Such people can perceive a quiet controlled voice as passive even when in fact it may be extremely assertive.

> With its strong emphasis on competition, Western culture champions the strong over the weak. Aggression is encouraged in everything from school contact sports to business take-overs.

But there is another way for human beings to

interact. We can use verbal problem-solving skills. Until recently few of us in Western cultures had developed the skills needed to use them. With its strong emphasis on competition, Western culture champions the strong over the weak. Aggression is encouraged in everything from school contact sports to business take-overs. The passive approach is for weak 'wimps'. However, while this may have been wonderfully successful in the short term for business and the 'economy', it's no way to behave if you want successful long-term relationships or a successful long-term economy.

Sooner or later, in order to defend themselves and their human dignity, passive people become passively aggressive. Passive aggression occurs when you say nothing openly but you just don't co-operate fully, or you 'throw spanners in the works' to mess up things in such a way that it is difficult to lay blame.

For instance, a passive spouse who has an aggressive, abusive partner may give 'the silent treatment', sulk, refuse to do jobs around the house that are normally their responsibility, be deliberately late and keep their spouse waiting.

In the workplace the passive–aggressive worker can make deliberate mistakes, go slower, be unco-operative about change, give away company secrets, petty-pilfer, or even deliberately sabotage the company.

In the long term, human beings and businesses need to develop better verbal problem-solving skills that respect the rights of all parties. This is called assertiveness.

Before you can use the verbal problem-solving skills of assertiveness you need to adopt certain beliefs. In his book *When I Say No I Feel Guilty*, Manuel Smith describes ten rights people need to claim as beliefs in order to effectively stand up for themselves. (This book is one of the easiest to read on the subject and goes into more detail than is possible here.)

For situations where there is relative inequality between you and somebody else, for example family, friends, other adults and colleagues, and for those whose religious beliefs run counter to the idea of equal rights between men and women, use this information according to your own discretion.

Bill of Assertive Human Rights

I. **You have the right to judge your own behaviour, thoughts and emotions and to take the responsibility for what they are and their consequences.**

This is basically saying you have the right to take control and manage each step in the chain reaction we talked about on pages 16–65.

Many people give to others the right to judge: their parents ('father/mother knows best'), spouse or anyone other than themselves. Decide this moment to claim that right for yourself and you'll be free from having to constantly please other people and feeling guilty if you don't.

2. **You have the right not to justify your behaviour by offering excuses or reasons.**

As an adult you are not answerable to other people for your beliefs or your actions (unless they impinge on other people's rights and freedoms, or they are against the law!). You are no longer a child having to answer to parents and teachers and being obliged to justify your actions.

Next time someone asks you to do something you don't wish to do or can't, try saying 'I'm sorry, I can't help you' and STOP. Don't make excuses. It's a wonderfully liberating feeling.

3. **You have the right to decide the degree to which you are responsible (if at all) for finding solutions to other people's problems.**

Ultimately each person must take appropriate responsibility for their own feelings, behaviour, pain, health and so on. You may be able to temporarily please someone by altering your behaviour to suit them, but over the long term this simply undermines *your* self-respect and stops *them* from taking responsibility for their own actions and lives.

Denying this right of a person also happens when responsibility for a problem is shifted onto the victim: you make a legitimate complaint and an organisation accuses you of being unreasonable, denies responsibility or tells you to see the subcontractor they organised to do the job. Or a victim of abuse is told by his or her tormentor that if the victim changed their ways they would not be abused.

When you make a complaint you upset people, and if they don't handle that complaint appropriately the first thing they do is accuse you of being a troublemaker. Unfortunately, the average person falls for this hook, line and sinker, and is made to feel that the problem would go away if only they would simply shut up and disappear.

4. **You have the right to change your mind.**

Circumstances change, people change, you change. Changing your mind does not imply incompetence, inadequacy or indecision. It indicates that you are flexible enough and confident enough to claim the right to reassess something and change accordingly. This flexibility is a virtue, not a fault (unless you have a real problem making any decisions).

5. **You have the right to make mistakes and be responsible for the outcome.**

If you discover you are wrong, the most assertive thing you can do is to claim the right as a human being to make mistakes and take action to correct them.

If someone is criticising you or pointing out a mistake, claim this right by saying 'You're quite right. I'm wrong'.

If you are quite comfortable with the idea of being wrong, the other person's attack collapses. If you are responsible for a situation with a disastrous outcome, forgive yourself with the thought: 'I did what I could at the time'.

If, however, you are being criticised or attacked but you don't agree you are wrong, use words such as 'probably', 'could be', 'perhaps' or 'maybe': 'Perhaps you've got a point ...'; 'You could be right ...'; 'Maybe you're right ...'; 'You probably have a point ...'; 'I hadn't thought of it like that ...'

These phrases give recognition to the other person's viewpoint, which takes the heat out of the situation but retains your right to have a different opinion; to agree to disagree.

The criticism may be general and aimed more at deliberately undermining your self-acceptance: 'You look like you've put on weight'; 'That colour really doesn't suit you'; 'You're so aggressive'.

Acknowledge their opinion, but keep asking for more information so they have to keep justifying their comments and you appear totally unconcerned but genuinely interested in their comment.

Friend:　You look like you've put on weight.

You:　You might be right; what makes you think I have?

Friend:　Your hips look bigger.

You:　Do they? Do you think it's these pants, or the colour or is it actual weight?

Friend:　Well, it could be the pants, I suppose.

You:　I was wondering myself whether they were a good choice. Thanks for your opinion.

This approach is guaranteed (as long as you are not sarcastic and you look the critic straight in the eye) to give you a fantastic feeling of personal control and make the other person reluctant to ever try picking on you again.

6. **You have the right to say 'I don't know'.**

What a relief not to have to know everything!

You are now free to try things before you know all the answers, to experiment, to explore, to ask. As Huckleberry Finn realised, other people love showing you what they know, and if they can do so, let them. If you are really clever, you can stand back and let them help you a great deal while you stay quite comfortably ignorant and save your energy for more important things. This right also allows negative consequences for your actions. If you don't know everything, sometimes the consequences can be unexpected and unwelcome. But that's OK because you don't have to know everything.

7. **You have the right not to be liked by everyone you have to deal with.**

    It's very nice to be liked and approved of, but if you go around thinking that this is a prerequisite for dealing with people you may well find yourself being manipulated mercilessly as you try to please others.

    In fact the more people see you as your own person, willing to be pleasant but not needing approval, the more you will find them wanting to please you! Independence will make you attractive to others, who want to be approved of by someone they see as strong.

However, there are organisations that find such independence extremely threatening. They often have a highly authoritarian structure where power is claimed by people feeling that those under them have to grovel and please. If you are not prepared to play these games, get out of the situation if you can because you are a major threat to the whole way the organisation operates (see pages 149–155).

In ordinary person-to-person situations with people of equal standing, trying to please can mean you end up agreeing to lots of things you just don't like in order to avoid hurting their feelings. Remember – they are responsible for their feelings, not you!

8. **You have the right to be illogical in making decisions.**

My teenage son is an expert at finding weaknesses in my reasoning and arguments about why he should not do certain things. Worse still, he remembers what I said months or even years previously and has no difficulty pointing out that I am hopelessly illogical and inconsistent.

The fact that things are logical does not make them right, nor does it make them what you want. Take the right to do things and feel things because you want to, not because they are logical.

9. **You have the right to say 'I don't understand'.**

If you live or deal with people who expect you to be able to read their minds and automatically know what they want, when they want it and how, they can become very irritable and aggressive with you when you don't comply.

It's not your responsibility to work out what's going on in somebody else's head or to guess their needs. It's up to them to spell it out clearly. Put the responsibility squarely back with them to tell you what they want.

Sensitive people tend to expect this mind-reading from others because they may be good at intuitively responding to other people's needs. They assume this characterisitic in others, and its absence leads them to imagine lack of interest or caring. Really intuitively sensitive people, well tuned to others, are actually quite rare. Most people are too wrapped in themselves to use such sensitivity, even if they have it.

There are also some interesting basic differences between the way men and women communicate and these can cause misunderstandings. If in doubt, check it out! The book *You Just Don't Understand What I Mean* by Deborah Tanner explores these fascinating differences in gender communication.

10. **You have the right to say 'I don't care'.**

A rather nasty form of dogma has recently crept into a great deal of Western culture. It demands that everyone should be trying to improve themselves, whatever that means. Constant striving to improve yourself according to the dictates of a mythical perfection means the search is never-ending. The money keeps flowing into the 'personal development' business, but your enjoyment of life is suspended until you have sorted yourself out – the 'I'll be happy when ...' or 'I'll be happy if ...' trap.

None of us is perfect, nor did anyone have a perfect upbringing. If you are comfortable with and used to your 'hang-ups', and they don't impinge on the rights of others, then don't let anyone else bully you into getting rid of them. Often these 'hang-ups' are very important survival strategies that you have adopted for good reasons and need to hang on to until circumstances, or opportunity or time, allow you to change them to something more constructive.

On the other hand, you may resist changing yourself as a form of passive aggression in response to someone else's refusal to accept you as you are. Often the less someone is hassled about changing to what others think they should be, the more likely they are to change because it suits *them*. You can't change other people; you can only change yourself and your own behaviour. But that in turn can cause a chain reaction that *allows* other people to change too.

If you are being pestered by people telling you what you should or should not do, say to them: 'You might be right, but I don't care to change right now'; 'You may be right but I don't want/choose to change'; 'You might be right but I choose to do this in my own way'.

Knowing that you have the right to choose to be assertive if you wish is one thing; knowing how to do it is quite another. It's very important to realise that being assertive is a verbal problem-solving option to add to your repertoire of strategies for dealing with people. It is not always the right option for all people, of all religions or all cultures. It's up to you to choose this assertive option appropriately, according to your own values and your desire for particular kinds of relationships.

It is also important to remember that you will need to modify how you use these skills depending on the power differential between you and the other person and the organisational structure.

When you start using these skills and asserting your rights it will seem quite strange, like breaking in new shoes. There may be a few blisters to start with: people close to you may get quite angry and annoyed that they can no longer manipulate you the way they are used to or that your attitude and behaviour is no longer predictable. You therefore need to give some thought to the effect of the consequences of this assertiveness on personal and professional relationships. There can be advantages: as you feel better about yourself, other people tend to treat you with more respect and you attract people who operate in a more assertive way. However, some people may have a vested interest in keeping you as a doormat and will try very hard to undermine

> ✒ Being assertive does not mean operating in a way that is contemptuous of other people's feelings, but rather in a way that shows mutual respect. ✒

you. Think it through before you start. Are these people important enough in your life that you care whether or not they can cope with the changes?

Being assertive does not mean operating in a way that is contemptuous of other people's feelings, but rather in a way that shows mutual respect and your acceptance of only *appropriate* responsibility for other people's reactions.

The basic skills of standing up for yourself

The broken-record technique.   The easiest way to manipulate people is to distract them from the real issue. This is usually done by making them feel they are being unreasonable, or by using red herrings or attacking the person so they feel they have to defend themselves.

So to be assertive you need to be persistent and stay focused on the real issue. The broken-record technique works by forcing the other person to deal with the real issue and no other.

Let us explore the example of a customer returning a clock to a store after a hand fell off while it was being used for the first time.

Customer:	I bought this clock yesterday and the hand broke off the first time I wound it. I'd like my money back.
Sales assistant:	That is a very good clock; the hand couldn't just fall off. (*You are lying.*)
Customer:	The hand did just fall off, and I want my money back. (*Broken record.*)
Sales assistant:	We've never had this happen before. You must have overwound it or something. (*You are lying.*)
Customer:	No. The hand fell off. I'd like my money back. (*Broken record.*)

Sales assistant:	You'll have to contact the manufacturer. It's not our fault. (*Evasion of proper responsibility; you are being unreasonable expecting us to pay.*)
Customer:	You sold me the clock. The hand broke. I want my money back. (*Broken record.*)
Sales assistant:	Look lady, we didn't make the clock. We can't do anything about it. It's not our fault. (*Shifting blame; you are unreasonable.*)
Customer:	You sold me the clock. The hand broke. I want my money back. (*Broken record.*)
Sales assistant:	I'll get the manager.
Manager:	The hand wouldn't just break. My assistant has explained our policy and you are upsetting him. (*You're a liar, a nuisance and a bully.*)
Customer:	The hand broke and I want my money back. (*Broken record.*)
Manager:	Give her the money! (*We're not going to get anywhere with her.*)

Because of your sticking to the issue and not allowing yourself to get drawn into side issues or to be forced to defend yourself against attack, the sales assistant and the manager have to face the issue and solve the problem – you are obviously not going to give in! Your tone of voice is very important. The same words can be assertive or extremely aggressive. Practise a tone that is respectful of the other person and is therefore assertive.

The broken-record technique is also ideal when people refuse to take no for an answer. For example, sales techniques these days are more likely to consist of subtle methods to get a conversation going so that sales staff can discover your needs, fears, and any obstacles to a sale. So no matter what they might say, stick to the issue: 'I'm not interested'.

Saying no to friends can be more difficult as they may use emotional blackmail or issue veiled threats that your friendship will be jeopardised if you don't comply. If they do this, perhaps you'd be better without them as friends. Real friends will respect your right to say no and have limitations. Again, make sure your tone is assertive, not aggressive.

Friend: Could I borrow your car tomorrow while mine is being serviced?

You: No, I don't lend my car to anyone.

Friend: What, not even me? (*You don't trust your friends; I'm hurt.*)

You: It's nothing personal. I don't lend my car to *anyone*. (*Broken record.*)

Friend: Well, after all the things I've done for you! (*You're ungrateful.*)

You: I appreciate the things you've done for me, but I don't lend my car to anyone. (*Broken record.*)

Friend: Some friend you turned out to be! Anyway, everyone says you're selfish! (*Distraction; personal attack to induce guilt.*)

You: I'm sorry you feel that way, but I don't lend my car to anyone. (*Broken record.*)

('Friend' leaves in a huff.)

After an exchange like this you can feel upset that your friend showed no respect for your right to say no, but you will not feel guilty: as you now believe you have a right to say no. The broken-record technique is necessary only when you feel that the other person is not respecting your needs or rights equally. It's a way of establishing your equal rights and self-respect in the exchange so that you come away feeling good about yourself.

However, if you feel there is genuine respect for your rights and needs, you can use other options.

Workable compromise. This allows you to choose to come up with a solution that will perhaps meet your needs as well as those of your friend. If your friend had to take his mother to the doctor when his car was being fixed, you might offer to give him a lift. You might even decide to lend the car for that specific period of time, feeling that since he respected your position he can be trusted.

Feedback on behaviour. Although you can't force people to be nice to you or to treat you with respect, letting them know how their behaviour affects you is an extremely effective and powerful way for you to assert your right to feel the way you do. At the same time, this 'When you do X I feel Y' formula gives other people feedback on the consequences of their behaviour. This can encourage abusive or difficult people to modify their behaviour. For example:

- 'When you speak to me that way, I feel you don't respect/love/like me.'
- 'When you ignore my requests for help, I feel you are taking me for granted/despise me/think I am your slave.'
- 'When you don't do your chores, I feel unappreciated.'
- 'When you don't clean up the bathroom after

yourself, I feel humiliated that you think it's OK that I have to use it in your mess.'

Even if your reactions are unjustified, your feedback gives the other person the opportunity either to change their behaviour or to reassure you that your interpretation is not their intention. Expressed calmly without condemnation, this is an extremely powerful way for couples, or teenagers and their parents, to develop better understanding and communication. But make sure that your tone of voice and your body language are neutral, otherwise what you say could come across as emotional blackmail.

Appropriate assertion.   Unfortunately men who are aggressive, bullying or unsure of themselves can read strong assertive behaviour in men as acceptable, but in women as aggressive. If this happens to you, think long and hard about your tone of voice, your body language and your choice of words. If in your own mind your behaviour is appropriately assertive, stick to your guns and realise that such a reaction in a man is a reflection of his insecurity or incompetence and not a reason for you to please him by becoming passive.

Of course, sometimes the reverse can be true. Women who claim to be assertive when they are actually rather aggressive can read men and women who stand up to them assertively as aggressive!

On the rare occasions that I have been accused of being aggressive, the accuser either has been someone not doing their job properly or had something to hide. Sometimes my assertiveness has quite unwittingly threatened them with exposure and/or accountability. If you stumble across a situation like this, an aggressive reaction to your appropriately assertive behaviour can be the first clue that there is something wrong.

Time management. Having personal control of your life also means managing your time well and learning to delegate responsibility. People who are busy with activities that satisfy them, and that are stimulating and challenging (but not overwhelming), are more likely to be happy. People who do not allow themselves to become involved in jobs or situations beyond their ability or skill level, but who also seek out opportunities to extend themselves in their leisure time, will also be happy.

> People who are busy with activities that satisfy them, and that are stimulating and challenging (but not overwhelming), are more likely to be happy.

Good time management does not mean cramming into a day more than anyone else in an effort to prove how important you are. The business executive who talks to a client while instructing his secretary, taking phone calls, reading faxes and drinking coffee is not impressing anyone. Rather he is displaying a disturbing tendency to let himself be controlled by outside demands. People in power need to have the personal strength and capacity to be in control of the situation and not have the situation controlling them. Besides, sharing the load doesn't just give you more control and make you happier; taking on more responsibility can help make other people happier too.

Happiness does not come from being busy for busy's sake; it comes from a degree of planning, which allows a sense of personal control, and which provides room for things to look forward to as well as joyful spontaneity.

Standing up for yourself in organisations

Once you come to believe and use the Bill of Assertive Rights, standing up for yourself in personal and day-to-day relationships can become fairly straightforward because of the relatively equal power operating between the two people concerned. However, standing up for yourself in hierarchical organisations can be quite another matter.

In the armed forces, the police force and many businesses, a strict hierarchical structure has to exist in order for the organisation to do its job properly.

In such organisations, there should be clear codes of conduct and accountability, and other strategies, in place to safeguard everyone against abuse, bullying and intimidation. The long-term strength and effectiveness of these organisations depends on the effective operation of these safeguards.

However, there are many organisations, particularly in business, where there are no safeguards operating other than those imposed by government regulations, for example anti-discrimination legislation, and occupational health and safety regulations.

People working in such organisations can have a hard time protecting their rights and keeping their jobs. Ultimately, each individual has to decide what their limits are and choose either to put up with the status quo, to complain or to leave. Unfortunately, far too often people have to face the reality that in complaining they may lose even if they win, for example when the woman who successfully brings a case of sexual harassment finds that the ill feeling is such that she cannot return to her job.

Ultimately, each individual has to decide what their limits are and choose either to put up with the status quo, to complain or to leave.

In these situations, think very carefully and explore all the options before taking action.

Organisations and office politics

Office politics is often associated with dirty, manipulative game-playing used by those in power, those who want to get more power, and those who want to control power in organisations.

Unfortunately, this image can inhibit a lot of extremely competent people, especially women, from rising to the top in organisations because they don't want to get their own hands dirty or to grovel.

But office politics also involves recognising that in any group of people there is a constant (and normal) jostling process going on while people continue to work together with a common aim. Where there is good management, there is genuine empathy, respect and courtesy shown towards other people, which makes this a constructive process. Destructive office politics occurs in organisations that are obsessed with pitting one employee against another and where those at the top use secrecy, manipulation, bullying, intimidation and power to cover up for their own inadequacies both in management and in interpersonal relationship skills.

Unless you are fully prepared for the stress and are well supported by others with some kind of effective power, don't waste your energy trying to change such organisations, because the structure that is supporting such destructive practices will turn on you. Put your head down and do your job, but seek employment elsewhere as fast as you can.

In any organisation, however, you need to be aware of 'how the system works' in order to survive and thrive!

Consider the organisation's expectations, for example:

- How long do people work?
- What is the code regarding lunchbreaks, tea-breaks (if any), and dress?
- What is the policy on taking holidays (do people take them all at once, at certain times or in part to suit the boss?)?
- How do people address each other?

Then think about the formal organisational structure:

- Who answers to whom?
- What are the different roles and job specifications of different people?
- Who has the power to do what?

Understanding the informal organisational structure can be more important than knowing the formal network:

- Who talks to whom?

- Who lunches with whom?
- Who *really* has power in the organisation?
- Who socialises outside the office?
- Who has influential contacts (media, business, personal) outside the organisation?
- Who likes whom?
- Who is isolated or actively rejected?

Gatekeepers to power

These are the personal assistants and secretaries who are often inadequately paid and poorly recognised despite what they do, and are resentful because of it. This can make them difficult and manipulative, with a compulsion to exercise what little power they have by controlling who sees their boss. The long hours they spend with their boss can give them a professional and personal intimacy, with enormous influence over the boss's perceptions of different employees.

You have to get these people actively on your side or at least make sure they are not actively against you. As long as they don't see you as a threat to their boss and hence their own power, this is pretty simple to do by being polite and courteous. Recognise their power by asking for their opinion or help. A little bit of recognition can pay handsomely.

Be professional but human

Keep your professional life separate from your personal life by avoiding intimate relationships with staff. However, there are many jobs demanding mutual trust where. *appropriate* personal disclosure helps unite an organisation or team to make them far more effective, for example in teaching, the police force, hospitals and so on. But in general keep your personal life and problems at home.

Attending work social functions and mixing in the tearoom or staffroom are vital to keeping in touch with the organisational grapevine. Gossip and rumour are natural consequences of people's being together, and can be very constructive in bonding groups as they occur only when people are interested in each other. But don't engage in or encourage destructive gossip or rumour.

The office Christmas party can ruin promising career or job prospects. Remember you are 'on duty' at a Christmas party, where you can be more ruthlessly judged than in your professional 'role'. At a Christmas party you are perceived as being more 'the real you', so be on guard. Don't drink excessively, or at all if you can't tolerate alcohol. Don't get into heavy or 'deep and meaningful' conversations. Keep yourself pleasant and happy, and make only appropriate personal disclosures, for example your interest in butterflies, not your desire to be a wizard.

I've always seen office politics as simply being the task of getting on with people and having some sensitivity to and consideration of other people's needs as well as one's own. This approach seems to work extremely well and I have never needed to play games or stab people in the back.

However, I have dealt with organisations that had a highly manipulative bullying management, in which case I've either got out of the organisation as fast as possible or have had to stand up to the people concerned, while realising fully the personal and professional costs of doing so.

Office politics does not have to be a dirty game. Stand back and assess the situation carefully before deciding whether to stay or to leave. Be aware at all times that if an organisation plays dirty games and you try to go against this, you will probably be the loser: you are just too threatening for the more senior management to allow you to survive. Be satisfied, knowing that in the long term these types of organisations will destroy themselves anyway.

If you are lucky enough to have come in at the top or as a consultant to change a corporate structure, you may have to be ruthless and get rid of key personnel in order to change an organisation's destructive culture.

Don't ignore the politics of organisations. Instead become aware of and embrace them in a healthy, constructive way.

If you own a business or are responsible for employing consultants, clarify your short- and long-term objectives. Consultants have a vested interest in providing short-term solutions. As long as a consultant produces an illusion of short-term magic (that doesn't necessarily work in the long term), they will continue to be consulted. In the process they can create appalling human misery and devastating damage, particularly when hard-working and conscientious employees leave in disgust after watching deviousness and manipulation rewarded. Remember that happier workplaces enjoy less absenteeism and increased productivity. Inappropriate cost-cutting and 'downsizing' can create spectacular short-term profits, but spectacular long-term problems and losses.

If you are training managers, don't start with the wrong end of the stick. To develop people into managers who can create happier and healthier workplaces, it is far easier to sharpen the financial and business skills of genuine people than it is to teach natural interpersonal skills to cunning manipulators. Those doing the training must have real respect for and an interest in other people; cute phrases and rehearsed body language screams at people that they are being conned.

So don't ignore the politics of organisations. Instead become aware of and embrace them in a healthy, constructive way. If you are an employee, find an organisation that will allow you to reach your potential without sacrificing your personal integrity, making you a happier and more productive person. If you own a business, think about how you can create a happier and healthier work environment. It pays!

In short ...

- A sense of personal control is essential to your happiness, but don't make the mistake of thinking that you are in total control of (and to blame for) everything that happens to you.

- The other side of the coin is to not see yourself as a helpless victim, with zero influence over your life.

- Be aware, and develop a sound understanding, of the links between events, thoughts and feelings.

- It helps to say in your self-talk: 'I don't *have* to do this — I *choose* to'.

- Simplify your life by separating the essential from the unnecessary.

- Use the five ways to help you stop worrying.

- Don't allow yourself to become the 'fixer' for other people's problems. And don't be anybody's scapegoat.

- Establish clear and reasonable personal boundaries and stick to them.

- Claim the ten articles of the Assertive Bill of Rights — they are *yours*.

- Learn how to use the assertive option that respects you as well as others.

- Learn how to use office politics constructively.

The 4th Secret:
Happy people enjoy the doing

'Flow' theory

Early research into what makes people happy focused on whether people reported being happy or unhappy as if it were an off–on experience. However, in the early 1990s a happiologist called Csikszentmihalyi became interested in what made people feel really, really happy (what he called 'optimal experiences'). He observed artists and sculptors and noticed that they would become totally absorbed in their projects, focused entirely on what they were doing each second, each minute, each hour. When he talked to

> 🖋 We enjoy ourselves most and feel happiest when we are caught up in and totally absorbed with the 'flow' of an activity. 🖋

them it became apparent that the consequence or outcome of their work was not the motivator, nor was it what gave them their enjoyment. They reported

that the greatest feelings of happiness and the most pleasure were derived from the actual doing of the task, of being 'in the flow'.

By studying a range of people doing all sorts of different tasks, he discovered that happiness comes from doing things that are a 'mindful challenge', not from doing things that encourage only 'mindless passivity'. In other words, we enjoy ourselves most and feel happiest when we are caught up in and totally absorbed with the 'flow' of an activity. At these times we are not conscious of the self, and time flies.

Csikszentmihalyi discovered that:

- If you are doing activities that are highly challenging and you bring a low level of skills to the task, you feel anxious.
- If the task requires a low level of skill and has little challenge, you will feel apathetic.

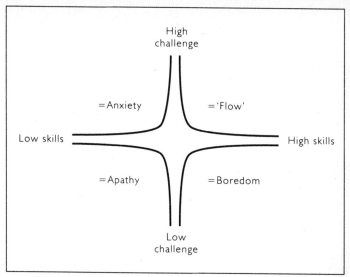

The 'flow' model

- Activities that require a lower level of challenge than your high level of skill will make you bored.

- But when you use a high level of skill to do highly challenging tasks, you can experience the total absorption and satisfaction of 'flow'.

Looking at experience in terms of the level of skills you have and the level required to do the task can help you to examine which parts of your life may be holding you back from experiencing optimal happiness.

Allowing yourself to 'flow'

More is involved than the demand characteristics of a task versus your ability and skill level. Your attitude towards the task and your ability (or your self-talk about them) can profoundly affect whether you are prepared to allow yourself to have an optimal 'flow' or really happy experience.

If you feel you don't deserve to be really happy, or if being happy makes you feel guilty, then even when opportunities arise to be extremely happy you will hold yourself back. In teenagers it's common to feel that it's not cool to be happy at school or ever to get on with teachers and adults generally. So even when teachers go to enormous lengths to try to provide the opportunity for 'flow' experiences in the classroom, the students may refuse to let it happen. Notice the differences in the effects that these pairs of statements have on your mind and body:

- 'This is a real challenge.'
  'This is too hard.'
- 'This will be the toughest, most hard-working year of your life.'
  'This will be one of the most stimulating, challenging and rewarding years of your life.'
- 'I can't do this.'

'This looks quite tricky but I'm sure I can figure it out or get help.'

- 'This is impossible.'

'I need some help.'

- 'I'll never get it done.'

'If I plan and manage my time well and focus on one thing at a time, I'm sure I'll get it done.'

Many words have the effect of shutting you down and making it difficult for you to think or use skills within yourself, or to seek help from others:

- can't
- impossible
- never.

Other words make you feel more relaxed and open to access your ability and that of others:

- stimulating
- challenging
- rewarding
- tricky.

Try using words in your self-talk that allow you to make use of potential optimal 'flow' experiences that call on your higher levels of skill in a task with a high level of challenge.

Allowing yourself to 'flow' with your responsibilities and roles in life also brings deeper satisfaction, with much less stress.

MARY AND BOB – A CASE STUDY

Mary and Bob were very conscientious parents who started a family in their late thirties. They tackled parenthood the way they tackled their jobs. They carefully researched and planned everything from conception, the birth, equipping the nursery and breast-feeding, to choosing toys, toilet training, diet and child-rearing ... Their expectations that they could plan and control parenthood quickly became unstuck when one child had severe colic from birth and the other was just a normal kid with his own agenda.

For Mary and Bob parenthood was something they would succeed at only if they and their children fulfilled a myriad expectations of what happened in 'happy' families. Their attempts to try to foresee and control every eventuality led to fierce conflicts with their children as teenagers and they complained in despair that their lives as parents of teenagers were preoccupied with the gruelling process of inevitable conflict.

What Mary and Bob hadn't realised was that parenthood is more like flowing and wallowing along while rowing down a winding stream, not speeding along a dead-straight river in control of a powerful motor boat going upstream.

If you allow yourself to flow along as parents with reasonable attempts to steer the rowing boat, you'll have a lot more fun (even if the rowlocks fall out occasionally) and really enjoy your kids. And you will be better role models.

All stages of being a parent can be wonderful. But sit back and rest occasionally and really cherish watching your children become separate, independent people with their own views, attitudes, strengths and weaknesses. Like rowing downstream, your role is to guide and influence, not control. Parenthood is not an endurance test; you are allowed to enjoy it while making human mistakes.

If you have difficulty letting yourself 'go with the flow', ask yourself if you feel you deserve to be really happy. Do you feel guilty about being happy? Staying miserable, apathetic or only mildly happy will not relieve other people's suffering or or the problems in the world. Besides, one person's happiness radiates happiness to others. Do you want to be responsible for sending out ripples of joy and happiness to others, or for sending out only ambivalence and misery?

> If you have difficulty letting yourself 'go with the flow', ask yourself if you feel you deserve to be really happy. Do you feel guilty about being happy?

Although each of us ultimately has to take responsibility for our own feelings, there is no doubt that interacting with happy, enthusiastic people tends to improve our own mood and vice versa. Every one of us can do our bit to improve the general level of happy, positive experiences by allowing ourselves to be happy first and then by radiating that optimistic, hopeful feeling to others.

So now I suppose you want to feel guilty for not feeling happy? If so, go back and read the section on self-talk (pages 46–60) and realise your right to feel and recognise your feelings no matter what they are (guilt included) before choosing what you would like to do about them.

Looking forward to the doing

It's not just enjoying the doing now that makes you happier and healthier, but also having new and different things to look forward to doing.

BILL AND SUSAN – TWO CASE STUDIES

Bill was eighty-five. He owned a beautiful property on which his family had farmed and grown orchards for generations. He had every illness associated with old age imaginable: heart disease, diabetes, chronic kidney disease, emphysema, arthritis, deafness and failing sight. But Bill was very happy. Like a set of rechargeable batteries, he just kept on going. As Bill put it, 'I've got too much to do and finish to die'. He restored old cars, and as he still had a shedful to restore, death wasn't an option. Despite his age he decided to rip out the apple orchard and put in a vineyard, as he'd always 'enjoyed a drop or two', and he was looking forward to his first vintage. He put in new plantations of trees and spoke of the future as if he fully expected to be around to see the trees mature in thirty to forty years.

Mary was forty when diagnosed with motor neurone disease. She had one of the most severe forms, one which usually results in death within two years. But at forty-five she was still alive, and although severely disabled, she was very much part of her loving family of five sons. Mary had been a keen gardener, and every time I saw her she had pots of bulbs coming up, in full bloom or dying off in her room. Just before becoming ill she had started experimenting with creating new varieties of daffodils, and watching how each new experimental flower would turn out had become a passion.

She would enthusiastically whisper to me in a voice almost gone with the disease about the colours and shapes she was aiming for. Her whole conversation was focused on future blooms which she had to be alive to see. Her husband and sons looked after the pots but she was in charge as only she knew how to care for them.

Mary's garden was on a very small scale but her

commitment to it and her curiosity about what would bloom next season gave her a powerful reason to live, which for many years slowed the progress of her disease.

It is perhaps not surprising that keen gardeners do seem to live to a ripe old age and appear to be a particularly happy lot. Many studies have shown a positive correlation between gardening and health and happiness. One particularly large study of 600 people concluded that gardeners enjoy better overall health, having fewer chronic health problems, making fewer visits to the doctor and even smoking less than non-gardeners. The more hours people spent gardening, the greater the effect, and those who spent five or more hours per week gardening were significantly happier.

Gardening combines many of the factors that promote health and happiness: enjoying the doing, commitment to something that depends on you, a sense of personal control, contact with others with common interest, an active outdoor lifestyle, stimulation and challenges appropriate to your skills and needs, structure and rhythm in your life, involvement with something bigger than yourself ('You are closer to God in the garden . . .'), and perhaps most significantly, having something to always look forward to.

Plan high points in your life to look forward to: something for each weekend, a night out occasionally, a new experience or challenge, but don't let yourself become obsessed by the future or with reaching goals – the 'I'll be happy or successful if ... when ...' syndrome.

> *Plan high points in your life to look forward to, but don't let yourself become obsessed by the future or with reaching goals.*

Appropriate goal-setting and planning will make you happier and healthier, but there is an alarming mantra being chanted in many personal development books and groups: that achieving goals is the be-all and end-all of a successful life. If you don't allow yourself to meander a bit, you will miss other opportunities for interesting side trips in life and you'll be going so fast towards your goals you'll miss the interesting scenery along the way.

A happier, healthier life comes from wandering the intriguing network of lanes towards interesting high points on the way to your long-term destination, not putting yourself on an expressway that you can't get off.

In short ...

- Ask yourself 'Am I prepared to allow myself to have a happy experience?' Let the answer be 'Yes!'

- Ask another question: 'Do I deserve to have happy experiences?' Again, the answer should be a resounding 'Yes!'

- 'Doing' brings pleasure and satisfaction, so get in the 'flow'.

- When you consider a task, think about the style of your self-talk. Avoid 'can't', 'impossible', 'never'. How about 'stimulating', 'challenging', 'tricky', 'rewarding' instead?

- Plan things to look forward to, and set appropriate goals.

- Don't make the goal the be-all and end-all. Remember the pleasures and the possibilities in the journey itself. Be open to the idea of wandering down intriguing byways.

The 5th Secret:
Happy people like people

Extroverts and introverts

People who seek the company of other people (extroverts) tend to be happier than those who don't or who deliberately avoid contact with others (introverts). The reasons for this and whether it is cause or effect are still rather unclear. It may be that if you are happy you are more likely to seek other people and become more extroverted, whereas if you are unhappy you tend to withdraw and become more introverted.

There is some research with twins that suggests that to some degree your capacity for happiness is inherited. But even if there is a genetic component, there are so many environmental and individual influences that can control or be controlled that this may not be as significant as it sounds. The research

Happy people enjoy people

suggesting a genetic component to happiness may well be actually measuring the genetic component of being an extrovert rather than an introvert or the genetic component of shyness and timidity. All these things affect the degree to which you will seek out and enjoy social interaction. Since a supportive network of family, friends and workmates is also related to the degree of health and happiness you feel, the genetic component may be a secondary rather than a primary factor.

As a clinician seeing children and adults, I would have to agree that people who are shy tend to avoid many situations and opportunities for enjoying happiness and, particularly, 'flow'. Shyness is very much an unrecognised disability, and unfortunately social disability is all but ignored in schools. Rather than receiving help, the shy child is more likely to engender frustration in teachers and bullying in other children, all of which makes the problem so much worse.

People who are shy:

- have difficulty in situations that are new or unfamiliar or in coping with changes: meeting people, making friends, trying a new experience or challenge;
- have difficulty standing up for themselves and expressing their opinions;
- tend to receive negative comments from others or be ignored rather than receive positive feedback;
- are extremely self-conscious and preoccupied with their own behaviour and thoughts, making it difficult for them to accurately perceive others or the situation;
- are highly anxious, so it is difficult for them to communicate effectively because they have trouble thinking clearly;
- have a tendency to engage in highly negative self-talk and hence be more prone to anxiety, depression and loneliness.

No wonder they are less happy than people who are easy-going extroverts! If you consider these features of shy people and the secrets of happiness we have been discussing, it is apparent that if you are shy, overcoming that shyness will do a great deal to help you feel happier.

Overcoming shyness

Shyness is extremely common but it does vary dramatically in degree. In one American survey 80 per cent of people said they had felt shy at some time in their lives. Of these people reporting the experience of shyness, 40 per cent felt they were presently shy and 25 per cent described themselves as chronically shy. But extreme shyness – where the person feels shy all the time in all situations with nearly all people – was reported by only 4 per cent of the chronically shy group.

Only 20 per cent of people in the survey described themselves as not being shy people but many of them still described having shy feelings in certain situations, for example experiencing blushing or a pounding heart when speaking in public.

Contrary to popular belief, being a shy child does

not necessarily mean you will be shy as an adult; nor does being confident as a child mean you may not become shy as an adult. Overall, men and women tend to report being shy equally, although it varies between the sexes at different ages. Adolescent girls tend to be more shy than boys the same age and young men more shy than young women. The fact that being shy can change so dramatically within the one person at different ages has suggested to a number of researchers and clinicians that if people wanted to be less shy then they could be helped.

It's important here to put in that proviso: if they *want* to change. Many shy people are very contented and happy about being shy. Their quiet, unassuming nature, which makes them tend to observe rather than participate, can actually free them from a great number of social and emotional demands and expectations. As they have no need to be the centre of attention, they can be non-threatening, easy company and good listeners. Because they don't attract or demand attention, they are free to be truly themselves. These people may well like solitude, enjoy their own company and not necessarily be lonely when alone. Quiet, shy people are often viewed socially as more sophisticated and charismatic because to a certain extent they appear to be untouchable.

However, for those who don't like being shy, whose self-consciousness compels them to sit on the sidelines when they would rather participate, who do feel lonely rather than merely alone, overcoming that shyness can make a huge difference to their enjoyment of life, their degree of happiness and their health.

Those people who are bothered by their shyness report three general types of symptoms that upset them:

- The behaviour that reveals to others that they are shy. This is not necessarily being unnaturally quiet or ill at ease when speaking but can reveal itself in being a 'motormouth' that can't keep quiet, or in extreme behaviour as an outlet for terrible anxiety. Very shy people find direct eye contact virtually impossible.
- The physical symptoms, including palpitations, sweating, blushing.
- The overpowering feeling of embarrassment and obsessive self-consciousness.

Instead of thinking of the good things that may come out of an activity or meeting, or focusing on the activity itself, shy people focus totally on themselves. If you think back to the chain reaction of perceptions, beliefs, thoughts, feelings and behaviour, you can see how this total focus on themselves can itself create and maintain the shy feelings. Focusing too much or exclusively on yourself tends to dramatically distort your perceptions of what is actually happening. You just don't see or hear anything but yourself.

If you have labelled yourself (or if others have labelled you) 'shy', a whole set of self-fulfilling beliefs is attached to that label. These beliefs about shy people in turn affect your self-talk, the situation and other people, and create physiological responses.

> Focusing too much or exclusively on yourself tends to dramatically distort your perceptions of what is actually happening. You just don't see or hear anything but yourself.

The physiological responses experienced by shy people may be identical to the flight-or-fight responses, which include sweating and palpitations. If you experience such responses, it is important to ask yourself why you are frightened. Are you frightened of rejection? of looking foolish? of making mistakes? Look at your self-talk about these fears because your self-talk will determine what you feel; for instance, embarrassment, hurt, rejection. These feelings affect your behaviour and so the whole cycle starts again. With each experience that triggers a cycle leading to embarrassment you become more and more reticent. Reticence occurs when you decide the effort you put in is not worth the outcome so you increasingly avoid situations that will set off the chain reaction that leads to anxiety and embarrassment.

If you want to overcome either chronically shy feelings or feeling shy in particular situations, you must tackle each link in the chain reaction of your responses to certain triggers.

As you start to look at your chain, it's worth realising that shy people characteristically judge themselves and other people quite harshly and tend not to give themselves the right to need or ask for help.

In order to tackle your general shyness or shyness in particular situations, you need to fully understand and be confident in applying what has already been discussed in this book.

Shyness specific to certain situations

There are a number of steps you need to take in order to confront and overcome shyness that is situation-specific:

Identify the situation. First of all, identify quite specifically what the situation is, for example public speaking.

Reframe the situation and reprogram yourself. Think about the first time you ever felt embarrassed speaking to anyone and write down the chain reaction that occurred as well as you can remember. For example:

Situation:	'Show and Tell' at school.
Perception:	Some people aren't listening to me. Some are talking to each other and laughing.
Belief:	They should be listening to me and looking interested.
Self-talk:	They are laughing at me! What's wrong with me? Do I look funny? Is my voice funny? Do they think the mushrooms I brought to show them are silly? I'm no good at this. They won't like me anymore.
Feelings:	Anxious, self-conscious, embarrassed, rejected, fearful of future rejection.
Behaviour:	Fidget, voice is shaky, start to sweat, go red, heart pounds. Stop talking and run to my desk.

Now go through that experience again but with the knowledge and resources you have now and alter the movie to something more realistic that recognises your rights and self-acceptance. For example:

Situation:	'Show and Tell' at school.
Perception:	The kids who always talk aren't listening, but are talking and laughing about something. Some kids look really interested.

Some are quiet but don't look interested.

Belief: It would be easier if everybody was listening and the teacher controlled them better.

Self-talk: These kids never listen to anyone. Some of the other kids look really interested, so I'll talk to them. I can cope with not being interesting to everybody.

Feelings: Annoyed that others are messing around and making it harder to concentrate. Pleased that those I am talking to are really interested and trying to see my mushrooms. Some are quiet, but it's OK if they're not interested in my mushrooms.

Behaviour: Focus on showing and telling about the mushrooms to those that are interested.

Do this with as many instances as you can remember that have caused shyness in the situation you have chosen.

Adjust the label. Consider what you say to yourself that maintains the label 'I am shy when ...'

How could you change that label or discard it completely? For example, if you say to yourself 'I've always been shy at public speaking', think about saying 'I am practising becoming more and more comfortable when I am doing public speaking so that I enjoy it more and more. I realise not everyone will be interested in what I say all the time, and I can be comfortable with that'.

Consider the positives and negatives of being shy.   Here you need to be very honest with yourself because often a particular label or behaviour is maintained because of its hidden benefits.

List all the negatives and positives (to both yourself and other people) of your being shy in that situation. For example:

Positives to me:	*Positives to others:*
• Don't have to make speeches.	• Others get the more important jobs.
• Get out of positions of responsibility.	• Others get to go away to conferences.
• People don't hassle me to be involved.	• Others who aren't as able get promoted ahead of me.
• People don't expect me to do presentations at work.	
• Don't get promotions so don't have to move interstate.	

Negatives to me:	*Negatives to others:*
• Hold back my career.	• Don't earn as much as I could and this puts more strain on the family.
• Don't get the credit for work I have really done.	
• Feel a wimp.	
• Do work below my ability level.	
• Feel inferior to people I know are less able but who can make speeches.	

You now have to decide how much you *really* want to change. Many people who complete this task are surprised at how strongly they either do or don't want to change! If your shyness suits you, stay with it until you feel it is something you want to change for yourself – not for your spouse or for your boss.

Improve your skills.   If you decide you really want to change, ask yourself if you have the skills you need. Although confidence and ability in dealing with most situations come with practice, improving your skill level and finding out the 'tricks of the trade' – be it in social situations (see page 272), speech writing or public speaking – can give you a huge boost in confidence and bring you into contact with other beginners able to support you as you support them.

If you need to improve your skills, find an appropriate teacher or group to develop these skills. If you have to play social golf or tennis as part of your business networking, at least have some lessons!

Desensitise yourself. This is a process by which you start with a totally comfortable situation and progressively work towards your goal in manageable steps.

If your goal is confident public speaking, a good way to start is to speak to a blank wall. If you can speak to a blank wall you will have no trouble when it comes to people, because you will not be dependent on the reactions of an audience. This makes it easier to focus on what you are saying rather than on yourself. When you do have an audience, focus on connecting with those people in the audience (there are always at least a few) who want your recognition as faces in a crowd and want to interact with you as you speak. They can be identified easily because they tend to sit up straight on the edge of their seats, try to get eye contact, and have pleasant smiling expressions.

Occasional speaking into a mirror can help you identify any unconscious mannerisms that you would like to modify. But don't speak into mirrors too much, as you tend not to focus on the task.

Depending on the particular situation you want to feel more comfortable in, joining a group of other beginners is a very good way of quickly desensitising yourself because you will be with people who have a common goal.

And don't feel that there is no discomfort on the way to feeling more comfortable! *Sometimes in life you have to summon the courage to move out of your comfort zone and take a few risks in order to challenge yourself and master new things.* The critical factor is engagement in self-talk that recognises your degree of discomfort but empowers you at the same time. For example: 'I haven't done this before so it will feel a bit strange at first, like new shoes, but soon I will feel more and more comfortable with this task. Even if I get blisters, they can heal and I'll be tougher, stronger and more skilled than before'.

Generalised shyness

If you have a more generalised shyness, the process is similar; but it can actually be easier because there are so many more opportunities to practise and become desensitised.

Be specific.   Identify the first time you can remember being shy, and particularly any fears you experienced.

Reframe and reprogram the chain reaction.   Write down the chain reaction that occurred, moving through perceptions, beliefs, self-talk, feelings and behaviour (see page 16).

Then reframe and reprogram this chain reaction, using all the skills and resources you have now that you are older. Deal with your initial fears, and use a more appropriate style of self-talk. Do this exercise for as many instances of shyness as you can remember clearly — even if this is a hundred!

Explore the labels.   Explore the labels you have given yourself over the years, or that other people have given you, and challenge their validity.

Become aware of what you have done that has given out signals to others that you were shy, and consider how this affected their attitude towards you.

Consider the positives and negatives of being shy.   Do the same exercise as before to discover how motivated you really are to change. If you do want to change, this will help you get a clearer idea of why you no longer wish to be shy. You may discover that you wish to retain some degree of shyness but just want to be less shy and more able to do things you have felt your shyness prevented you from doing in the past.

Think quite carefully about the degree of shyness or quiet reserve that would suit you.

Model yourself on someone you admire. Picture yourself not being shy. What would you do differently? How would you stand, walk, talk; in what position would you place your head; where would you be looking; what would your hands be doing?

The quickest way to feel differently is to act differently. Imagine someone you know or admire either personally or as a public figure, who displays the kind of social ease you would like to feel yourself.

Imagine watching that person closely, and become aware of each body movement. Now imagine yourself standing just behind them so you see the whole world as they would see it. How are people reacting to them? How does your model respond in turn? Again notice their body movements as they respond to other people.

Now imagine yourself stepping inside your model so that you not only see what they see but feel and hear what they experience as well. Get in touch with what it feels like to be your perfectly at-ease model.

To begin with you may like to imagine yourself as that person when you socialise, like taking on a role to play. This can be wonderful fun and you can amaze yourself at how instantly at ease you can feel. You will surprise yourself with the repertoire of skills that you have been absorbing subconsciously from others for years and can now find yourself using quite naturally.

As you become more and more comfortable with this role you will come to find more and more of yourself coming through, and soon you have the confidence and social ease of your model, but with your own special personality.

When you practise the new you, people who know you well, such as family and friends, will tend to expect you to behave in a certain way and may well make disconcerting comments such as 'What's happened to you?' or will make subtle attempts to keep you the way you were, because that's what they know and are comfortable with.

To make it easier, first try your modelling on strangers and in new situations: shopping, a new hobby or sport, classes. These strangers will have no preconceived ideas and hence readily accept the new you, giving you greater confidence and freedom to experiment.

If you feel you need more help to conquer shyness, see a psychologist who uses the 'switch technique'. This can be an extremely effective, quick way to change old ways of operating. You really *can* be more comfortable socially.

In short ...

- ❧ Think about this: is it that happy people like other people, or that liking other people helps make you happy?

- ❧ Shyness is a social disadvantage only if you worry about it or if it prevents you from doing things you want to do. Quiet, self-contained reserve has its advantages if you are prepared to explore the possibilities.

- ❧ If you have labelled yourself 'shy', or allowed someone else to do it for you, be aware of the self-fulfilling beliefs attached to the label. They will affect your self-talk to your disadvantage.

- ❧ Remember, shy people focus entirely on themselves. This does not leave them free to think about others or about the good things that might come out of encounters or activities.

- ❧ Identify any fears you have about mixing with people. Be specific, and then deal with them.

- ❧ Look at each link of the chain reaction – perceptions, beliefs, feelings and so on – in terms of your shyness. When you've identified each of them, tackle them one by one.

◊ Decide how much you really want to change. Maybe being shy suits you and you are trying to change only to please someone else.

I have now revealed the secrets of happy people: optimism, self-acceptance, personal control, doing things that provide adequate challenge and demand a high enough level of skill and social ease.

Acting happy makes you feel happier, and allowing yourself to enjoy *this very moment*, without focusing on the past or the future, leads to happier minutes, happier hours and a happier life.

In the next section we look at the secrets of healthy people and how being a healthy person is entwined with being a happy person.

PART THREE

Secrets of Healthy People

The 6th Secret: Healthy people like themselves enough to have a healthy lifestyle

Valuing yourself

How much do you value yourself? How well we look after ourselves is often a good indication of how much we value or like ourselves.

Depressed people tend to feel helpless and hopeless about their lives and this can be reflected in a general 'don't care' attitude to themselves emotionally and physically. In this condition personal hygiene can be allowed to deteriorate.

> ☙ The more you behave in a certain way, the more you will feel that way. ☙

People who look after themselves and who take pride in their personal hygiene and grooming, without being obsessive, give a message to others that they like and respect themselves. And as we have learnt, the more you behave in a certain way, the more you will feel that way.

Some of the most startling examples I have seen of changing behaviour causing a change in feelings have been in programs that take young, long-term-unemployed men and women and give them a one-week course in good grooming, personal hygiene, and presentation skills such as walking, standing, conversation, table manners, interviewing techniques, diet and so on.

The transformation in the appearance of these young people at the end of a week is staggering, but the way they felt about themselves was even more so. Their confidence, self-acceptance, self-liking and happiness just shone from their faces. They walked taller, spoke more clearly and firmly, and smiled, laughed and talked more. Many also found the real person they discovered hiding inside was now able to take on different interests and friends. Their new confidence helped them find work more easily and feel more motivated to adopt a healthier lifestyle.

Balancing your life

So to be healthier and to *feel* healthier, start to do what healthier people do. The lifestyle factors found to be most important for a long and healthy life are now well known:

- healthy eating
- exercise
- no smoking
- moderate alcohol consumption.

Healthy eating

The very word 'diet' creates so much unhelpful self-talk and feelings of failure, coercion, restriction, self-loathing, anger, frustration and so on that I now use the expression 'healthy eating' instead. I strongly recommend that you eliminate the word 'diet' from your vocabulary too.

Healthy eating is easier if you like yourself enough to want to take good care of yourself. If in the past you have had trouble eating well most of the time, have a good think your answers to the following questions:

> *Healthy eating is easier if you like yourself enough to want to take good care of yourself.*

- 'What is preventing me from eating well?'
- 'What would need to happen or change for me to be eating healthier food?'

Starving is not the answer. If you are on the large side, there is overwhelming evidence that counting calories

to lose weight will almost certainly make you fatter in the long term.

Starving by reducing calorie intake causes the body to slow down its metabolism, so it gets harder and harder to lose weight the longer the calorie restriction continues. This is worse if you don't get adequate and appropriate exercise. Paradoxically the more often you eat, the more calories you burn. If you restrict the number of times you eat as well as the calories, and you don't exercise, the limited weight you lose tends to be muscle tissue rather than fat tissue.

Muscle tissue has a higher metabolic rate than fat tissue, so over time you end up with a much greater proportion of fat to muscle in your body and a much slower metabolism; that is, more blubber and less muscle. Hence you tend to put weight back on much more easily. This yoyo-ing can permanently decrease your metabolic rate, making you even more prone to weight gain. In many ways it's better to not even lose weight in the first place than to get on this yoyo cycle.

Using food for comfort. There are a myriad emotional and psychological reasons why some of us overindulge most of the time, and in the wrong foods. Perhaps the most common are depression, poor self-acceptance and poor assertion skills.

If depression is a problem, overeating sugary and fatty foods (for example cream buns, cakes, lollies and deep-fried take-aways) can actually be a way of trying to 'self-medicate'. A diet rich in these foods and low in lean protein foods can increase the transport of tryptophan into the brain. Tryptophan is an amino acid needed in the production of serotonin. Serotonin is an extremely important brain messenger or 'neurotransmitter' vital for feeling happy and having good-quality sleep.

If you suspect emotional or psychological problems are inhibiting healthier eating, look at these issues first before trying to radically change what you eat. Reread the appropriate sections in this book or see a psychologist experienced in treating eating disorders.

In a small but significant number of people there are strong genetic influences on weight gain, and fat deposition and distribution throughout the body. These factors should not be ignored and they come into the issue of self-acceptance. However, they are often overplayed and used as an excuse to avoid facing more important factors causing poor eating habits.

Eating enough but not too much. Even if you don't have significant emotional reasons for overeating, there are a number of bad habits and wacky thinking practices that can tend to make you overeat.

If you allow yourself to be guided by the following suggestions, you will find it much easier to eat according to your body's real needs:

> ~ Learn what is food for the body and what is food for the soul! ~

- Eat only if you are hungry. This may mean learning

what true hunger is! Not boredom, tension or loneliness but real stomach-gurgling hunger.

- Eat in a calm environment with no distractions. It takes time for the messages from your stomach, saying it is full, to get back to the brain. If you eat in a rushed, tense environment, you often don't even realise when you've had enough.

- Eat what you want until you feel pleasantly satisfied. Listen to what your body really feels it needs (even some junk occasionally), not what you emotionally crave. Learn what is food for the body and what is food for the soul!

- Eat as if there are other people watching you. This stops you stuffing down food in a rush and binge eating.

- Allow yourself to eat what *you* want regardless of pressure and opinions from other people.

- Make eating a sensual experience by allowing yourself to relax and completely enjoy food, using all your senses: sight, taste, smell, hearing and touch. Take time to set the table, use attractive cutlery and china, soft lighting and pleasant music.

It's not how much you eat but what you eat. Rather than the amount you eat, sufficient aerobic exercise and an eating pattern that includes foods high in fibre and low in fat and salt are essential for maintaining a good body weight for your genetic make-up and basic body shape. You may still occasionally have rich decadent food but the general balance should be high-fibre and low-fat and salt.

People who need to lose weight should aim to have at least 30–40 grams of fibre and 30–40 grams of fat (see below) in what they eat each day, as well as making sure they get three half-hour sessions of aerobic exercise per week.

There are booklets available in bookshops and newsagents that list the fat and fibre content of fresh as well as name-brand foods.

If your weight is about right, to maintain it you need at least 30–40 grams of fibre a day and each day the following amounts of fat:

- women and children 30–50 g
- men 40–60 g
- active teenagers and very active adults 70 g
- hard manual workers and athletes in training 80–100 g.

Babies and children need proportionally higher fat than adults because their central nervous systems and bodies require fat for normal development.

An eating pattern low in fat and high in fibre also helps normalise blood cholesterol and triglyceride levels and decreases the risk of high blood pressure, bowel and breast cancer, gallstones and diabetes.

The best fats are monosaturated (not saturated or polyunsaturated; however, some saturated and poly-unsaturated fats — safflower and sunflower oils, milk, nuts, butter, cheese — should also be included in your diet). These are found in lean meats, fish and chicken, and in oils such as olive, macadamia and canola. Cold-pressed oils are better because they also contain certain natural anti-oxidants.

Foods high in fibre tend to be those that have had little processing, such as grains, lentils, vegetables, fruits, breads and cereals. Seeds and nuts are also high in fibre and contain the better mono- and polyunsatu-rated fats. They are rich in minerals and vitamins as well. Different types of fibre in foods give different benefits, so it is important to get your fibre from a wide variety of foods, for example grains, cereals, fruits and vegetables.

Too much fibre (more than 50–60 grams) each day is not a good idea because the fibre can interfere with the absorp-tion of some nutrients.

Healthier eating is really about being kinder to yourself!

The trick is *balance*. Many people become obsessed with what they eat each day. If you start thinking of the overall balance over two days it becomes much easier and more natural. So if you go out and have a very rich meal, just be kinder to your body over the next day or so.

Healthier eating is really about being kinder to yourself!

Exercise

For years we have been told about the benefits of aerobic exercise for our bodies and particularly for our hearts. (Aerobic exercise is the type that makes muscles work at a constant rate using a steady supply of oxygen.) But it has now been discovered that exercise makes you not only healthier but happier too.

Until recently it was thought that to get the physical and emotional benefits of exercise you needed to do some form of aerobic exercise three times a week for half an hour each time: five minutes of warm-up activity, twenty minutes of sustained exercise that continuously elevates the heart rate, and five minutes of cooling down stretches and exercises.

Aerobic exercise encourages the growth of small blood vessels called capillaries, improving the blood supply to the cells. It also increases the size and number of energy-producing units within muscle cells so that the ability to use oxygen is improved.

The heart rate becomes slower as the heart muscle

becomes thicker and stronger, which means greater efficiency and less effort in pumping blood around the body. In people who exercise regularly there is less incidence of heart disease and strokes, as well as fewer hip fractures due to osteoporosis.

Regular aerobic exercise also improves self-confidence and optimism and reduces feelings of helplessness, anxiety and social withdrawal. Exercise can be more effective than tranquillisers in reducing muscle tension. One study found a twelve-week aerobic exercise program was more effective than psychotherapy or medication in alleviating mild depression. Regular aerobic exercise has also been found to increase the ability to handle emotional stress.

> ◠ Exercise can be more effective than tranquillisers in reducing muscle tension. ◠

It now appears, however, that more moderate exercise that makes you a bit out of breath and warms you up, done for half an hour five times a week, is just as effective as aerobic exercise done three times a week.

Whether the exercise helps for purely psychological reasons, for example you feel more in control and therefore better, or whether there are physical changes with exercise that elevate mood, is not yet clear. The explanation is probably a combination. Exercise is known to elevate the body's production of its own opiates, which are natural substances produced by the body that are closely related (chemically) to morphine, heroin and codeine. With regular hard aerobic exercise the general level of these substances in the body is raised, making you feel good or even 'high'. Athletes who have to stop training suddenly due to injury can suffer from withdrawal, because these opiates are no longer being produced to the same degree. This gives them physical and emotional symptoms (irritability, depression) similar to those of withdrawing heroin addicts.

The best exercises are brisk walking, swimming, cycling, low-impact aerobics, rowing and cross-country skiing. Skipping and running are hard on joints and tendons if done regularly.

So to feel happier and healthier, start a program of exercise – either hot and sweaty three times a week, or warm and a little breathless five times a week. If you are over thirty or have health problems, check with your doctor first.

No smoking

There are a number of ways in which people stop smoking: through acupuncture, hypnosis or nicotine patches, by gradually reducing consumption or by just

> By honestly assessing your need to keep smoking, you can work out what may need to change in order for you to give up.

quitting. No method has been found to be superior to any other; it's really a matter of personal choice. However, there is no doubt that to stop any kind of substance abuse *you* have to want you to stop: not your doctor, your partner or your parents.

If you have tried unsuccessfully many times to give up, it's a good idea to ask yourself these questions:

- How would my life change if I gave up?
- What would need to change in order for me to stop?

In answering the first question, consider the *negative* as well as the positive consequences of stopping. You may be surprised by the hidden reasons that keep you smoking. (See list on page 203.)

By honestly assessing your need to keep smoking, you can work out what may need to change in order for you to give up. For example, you may need to:

- learn to relax without cigarettes
- learn how to be more assertive with others
- deal with problems you keep avoiding
- claim the right to still have time and money for yourself.

If people do this preliminary work before actually giving up (by whatever method they choose), their likelihood of success is much higher.

Positive changes:

• Be able to smell and taste again.

• Be healthier and have more energy.

• Feel in control.

• Others would no longer be able to read me and my state of mind by my smoking.

Negative changes:

• Lose something that calms me down.

• Might put on weight.

• Feel less sophisticated and in control.

• Have no excuse to go outside.

• Be giving in to my spouse's nagging.

• Be healthier so may be expected to do more.

• Wouldn't be able to rationalise the money spent on me.

Moderate alcohol consumption

Do you enjoy drinking alcohol as a pleasant relaxing pastime or are you driven to drink to cover up negative feelings you can't cope with?

If alcohol covers up bad feelings, you won't want to give it up until you find other ways of dealing with them. Answering the same questions just posed for smoking behaviour is also relevant if you want to modify your drinking.

Alcoholics Anonymous is adamant that alcoholics should completely abstain from drinking alcohol and while their program is successful, it is not suitable for everyone. You may prefer to learn to moderate and control your drinking rather than to abstain completely. Try these tips to modify your consumption:

> ✎ If alcohol covers up bad feelings, you won't want to give it up until you find other ways of dealing with them. ✎

- Don't drink alcohol to quench a thirst.
- Drink alcohol to enjoy the drink itself. Instead of 'Chateau Cardboard' and cheap plonk, buy a bottle of good-quality alcohol and enjoy it in moderation.
- Drink a glass of water after each glass of alcohol.
- Drink alcohol as an accompaniment to food.
- Drink socially, with people you like.
- Don't drink to cover up bad feelings. If you are depressed, or suspect you might be, seek proper medical and psychological help.

RICK AND ADAM – A CASE STUDY

Rick was thirty-two and extremely happy, with a stimulating and demanding job that he loved, a loving wife and two healthy children. He worked twelve hours most days and was interstate at least once most weeks.

Rick was very overweight. He had high cholesterol and high blood pressure, was a caffeine addict and maintained poor sleep patterns. He was very happy, but very unhealthy.

Adam was also thirty-two and with a loving wife and two healthy children. He exercised regularly, grew his own vegetables and was extremely careful about what he and his family ate. He was a non-smoker and an occasional drinker. He was very intelligent and extremely bored at work as a labourer since retrenchment from his middle management job two years previously. He was very fit and very unhappy.

Rick developed chest pains indicating early heart disease before he was prepared to look long and hard at his job and what it was doing to him. His own coping strategies weren't very good but the expectations of his employer were totally unreasonable. It came as a shock for him to realise that as far as they were concerned he could be easily replaced by someone else prepared to sacrifice themselves for the company.

Nursing a very bruised ego, Rick left and took a less exciting but also more realistically demanding job with another company. Although his health and coping strategies improved he realised he still missed the limelight and pres-tige of his previous job. But he also realised there were numerous organisations in the community willing to grab his skills on a voluntary basis and before long he found himself with a very high public profile in community service. He was soon happy *and* healthy.

Adam had to face the fact that his problem was boredom and loneliness. The small income did not bother him, so he too started to look around the community for ways to use his talent and skill and to network with people again.

His voluntary work with other unemployed people brought him into contact with many businesses in the area and within a few months he had not only a new network of friends, but also a part-time job in middle management again. He was now not only healthy but happy too.

To be both healthier and happier you need to achieve a balance between satisfying work and leisure time, and good-quality rest and sleep in your life.

In today's job market and with the totally unrealistic demands of many employers, this can be extremely difficult to achieve without being quite ruthless about your priorities. Unfortunately few people stand back and take a hard look at the balance in their lives until they are either very sick or very miserable.

> To be both healthier and happier you need to achieve a balance between satisfying work and leisure time, and good-quality rest and sleep.

It's a great pity that the egos of so many corporate chiefs prevent their seeing, or listening to, human resources personnel pointing out how destructive these jobs can be. A colleague in human resources in a large multinational company told me in despair that the company refused to accept the simple truth that two people each earning $50 000 and working a forty-hour week were infinitely more productive in the short and long term than one person working eighty hours per week for $100 000 a year.

If you feel a rumbling discontent with your life, stand back and see if the balance is right. Be honest about your real needs and explore ways that might possibly allow them all to be met.

As you rush around trying to meet deadlines and honour commitments, however, it is easy even to lose track of what these needs are, let alone to figure out how to

> ⚘ *If you feel a rumbling discontent with your life, stand back and see if the balance is right.* ⚘

meet them. Therefore it can be useful to first get in touch with the basics: what activities stimulate each of your five senses and make you feel good? This can give you immediate, daily access to lots of activities that can stimulate your own opiate system to make you feel immediately healthier and happier. In this way you can have regular time-out for pleasure throughout the busiest days.

Draw up your own personal pleasure chart like this one and indulge yourself several times a day by actually experiencing that activity or imagining it.

Sense:	*Feel-good activities:*
• Sight	• Sunlight through windows
	• Detail of a flower
	• Favourite view
	• Pictures of those you love
	• Monkeys, puppies, kittens playing
	• Dolphins surfacing
• Hearing	• Favourite music
	• Voice of someone you love
	• Sounds of the ocean
	• Bird calls
	• Wind in the trees
	• Chorus of frogs and cicadas
	• Children's voices in a schoolyard or at kindergarten
• Touch	• Feel of a loved-one's hair or skin
	• Silk or velvet

Sense:	Feel-good activities:
	• Sand under your feet at the beach • Hands stroking your hair • Massage, skin being stroked with a feather
• Taste	• Favourite wine • Favourite food • Salty taste of the sea • Crunchiness or smoothness of favourite foods
• Smell	• Smell of children's/baby's hair • Someone you love • Sea • Country • Mountain air • Favourite flowers • Loved pet • Favourite perfume • Wet gumleaves

It's not just the balance between work and leisure that is important but also the balance between activity and good-quality rest. Some people work too hard at leisure as well as at their job!

One of the most important lifestyle factors in health and happiness is a good night's sleep.

Sleeping well

It sounds so simple: a good night's sleep. But the refreshing and restorative feeling of a good night's sleep eludes many people. One in three people report significant sleep problems and about one in five complain they have chronic sleep problems.

> If you sleep well for an average of seven to eight hours each night, you are half as likely to become depressed as people who regularly sleep less, or more, than this amount.

If you sleep well for an average of seven to eight hours each night, you are half as likely to become depressed as people who regularly sleep less, or more, than this amount.

If you are not happy with the sleep you are having, the first thing to do is to work out the particular kind of sleep problem you have. It's very important to realise, though, that sleep varies through the night in a natural rhythm or cycle of very light to very deep sleep, so it is perfectly normal to nearly wake or actually wake several times a night. These are the times you usually roll over and change your position or get up and go to the toilet. Just realising that these waking moments are normal and then allowing yourself to drift back to deeper sleep can improve your sleep. But if you realise you are waking, saying to yourself 'I'm awake, I'll never get back to sleep' will condemn you to a very restless night.

During these periods of light sleep you are likely to dream, and you may have a nightmare. Your eyes move very rapidly, so this part of sleep is called rapid eye movement (REM) sleep.

Sleep problems are classified into three main groups with very different causes and solutions.

Sleep disorders of arousal

These disorders include sleepwalking, sleeptalking and the night terrors of children. If they occur in the first half of the night, they may well be temporary developmental problems that tend to right themselves in time. But if they occur in the latter half of the night, and particularly early in the morning, they may be due to an emotional upset of some sort. If the problem persists, some professional help may be worth considering.

Excessive daytime sleepiness

This almost always indicates either narcolepsy or sleep apnoea. Both conditions should be properly diagnosed and treated without delay.

Narcolepsy is genetic and usually starts in the teens. It is characterised by sudden attacks of sleep during the day, which may be triggered by emotion, a fright or excitement. It can be quite easily treated once diagnosed.

Sleep apnoea is a very serious medical condition more commonly found in older men. There are times when no air exchange occurs, so the sleep pattern is seriously disturbed because the person keeps waking to restore breathing. Very real oxygen deprivation can occur, causing heart failure and severe disturbances in psychological functioning, such as memory and concentration. Many patients are misdiagnosed as having Alzheimer's disease. Loud, irregular snoring with silent periods in between is the most obvious symptom, together with marked daytime sleepiness.

To diagnose this condition properly you will need a referral from your doctor to a sleep disorders clinic.

Insomnia

When most people say they are having difficulty sleeping, they are talking about either acute or chronic insomnia.

Acute insomnia can occur as a reaction to emotional or physical trauma and stress or as an after-effect of anaesthesia and surgery. In these cases mild medication for a few days *may* be advisable, although often it is better to let nature take its course and to allow the sleep pattern to be restored naturally.

Chronic insomnia is not satisfactorily treated with medication. It may develop slowly or as a result of an acute situation that has been inadequately resolved. Medication artificially alters the sleep cycle, often causing far worse problems in the long term. In some particularly sensitive people, disturbances in their natural sleep cycle have occurred months after taking pills for only a few days.

To help chronic insomnia, first of all consider how relevant the following factors are to your situation and then seek appropriate help or make the necessary changes to your sleeping routine.

Psychological factors.   Anxiety, unresolved conflicts, anger, resentment, depression, or psychotic illnesses, for example schizophrenia and manic depression, can all cause chronic insomnia.

Medical conditions.   Asthma, heart disease, lung disease, chronic pain, PMS, ear, nose, and throat infections or sleep apnoea. Have a physical check-up; especially have your thyroid function checked.

Drug side effects.   Prescribed medications (including unusual reactions to sedatives), alcohol, tobacco, and caffeine in tea, coffee, cola and chocolate.

Food / chemical / mould sensitivities.   If these are a factor, other physical or psychological symptoms will also be present. See your doctor for a referral to an environmental health doctor or see the bibliography (page 336).

Shift work and jet lag.   Both of these situations seriously disrupt natural daily body rhythms and sleep patterns by interfering with your eyes' exposure to ultra violet light. The same problem occurs in blind people. Light exposure regulates the body's production of melatonin, which controls these rhythms. Melatonin medication to correct the situation is now available in some countries.

Eating patterns.   Poor eating habits (including very large meals at night), junk foods (especially those high in sugar) and nutritional deficiencies. Do not take Vitamin B supplements at night, because they can disrupt sleep patterns by increasing your general level of arousal. A light snack before bed can improve sleep in people who have trouble maintaining adequate blood glucose levels through the night. L-tryptophan (available in health-food stores) is a natural amino acid that can help to shorten the time taken to get to sleep (sleep latency) because it stimulates the production of serotonin in the brain. Serotonin helps you get to sleep. A snack high in *complex* carbohydrate and low in protein can also increase the supply of tryptophan to the brain, for example a wholemeal bread salad sandwich and avocado.

If you suspect that your diet may be a problem, try eliminating all food additives, sugars and caffeine and lower your fat intake while increasing the amount of fibre you eat.

Timing of stimulation.   Too much stimulation (television, books, work) just prior to going to bed. Do not do hard aerobic exercise within four hours of going to bed. A gentle walk is OK. Hard exercise, especially outside during the day, stimulates much deeper sleep at night.

Physical conditions.   Noise, uncomfortable bedding, poor ventilation, extremes of temperature, street lights or other strong light sources, distracting decor of bedroom. Keep the bedroom for sleeping and for healthy sex! Keep television, computers, marital disputes and other stimulating activities out of the bedroom. If you are awake for over half an hour, get up and go into another room until you feel sleepy again. In that way your body and mind learn that *the bedroom is for sleeping*. Over time you actually learn to start to go to sleep as you walk into the bedroom.

If you have to study in your bedroom, have two clearly defined areas for working and sleeping. A desk lamp can be used as a cue: when the desk lamp is on, it's work time; when the desk lamp is off, it's sleep time.

Self-talk. Become aware of what you are saying to yourself about your sleeping habits. Good-quality sleep is as much an acquired habit as is a bad sleeping pattern. So you need to reprogram thoughts about difficulty in sleeping to allow a change in sleeping behaviour.

- If you keep saying 'I'll never get to sleep,' you won't!
- If you keep saying to yourself 'I'm not sleeping so tomorrow will be disastrous', it will be!
- If you say to yourself 'If I didn't have problem X

I could sleep', you won't sleep for as long as problem X exists.

Instead of using such destructive self-talk, try being a bit more realistic:

- 'In the past I've had difficulty getting to sleep but my mind and my body are now learning to sleep well.'

- 'At the moment I'm not asleep but I can lie here peacefully, imagining myself in a favourite place, and this is almost as effective as sleeping, so I will cope OK tomorrow.'

- 'Right now I don't choose to think about that problem. I'll deal with it in my worry time instead.' (See page 107.)

General relaxation. Lower your overall level of arousal by practising general relaxation techniques or deliberately doing relaxing activities a couple of times a day. Because your arousal will be generally lower as your sleep cycles vary during the night, you are less likely to actually wake up fully. It will then be easier to drift back into a deeper sleep.

A very simple relaxation technique is to sit comfortably wherever you are and do a brief body scan, moving either from the top of your head downwards or from your toes upwards. Adjust your position until you are as comfortable as possible, checking that your jaw, neck, shoulders, hands, legs and feet are not unconsciously tensed.

Then take a long, deep breath and say to yourself 'At this moment I can R-E-L-A-X'. Breathe out slowly, imagining any tension flowing out through your hands and your feet. A slow, even count of three in and three out gets the rhythm about right.

Another way to keep your general level of arousal lower is to find something that happens often in your daily routine to act as a relaxation reminder, for example the telephone ringing, going to the toilet, tea and lunch breaks. For instance, you decide to use the phone ringing as your relaxation reminder: instead of grabbing the phone on the first ring, take a deep breath and do the R-E-L-A-X exercise explained above. Then answer the phone and when you finish the call repeat the breathing exercise a few more times before continuing.

Working with your natural body rhythms will help you to achieve a balance between adequate sleep, rest, stimulation and pure pleasure (both physical and emotional).

In this way, at the end of your day you will be just as relaxed and calm as at the start of the day.

A number of studies have shown that what can be described literally as a day of REST (restorative environmental stimulation therapy) can dramatically affect

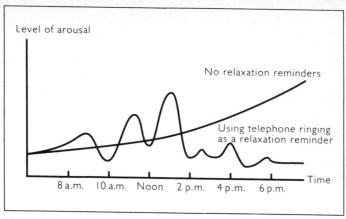

Using relaxation reminders

people's sense of wellbeing and personal control. In these studies, people lie quietly in darkened rooms with no stimulation such as reading, TV or music. The REST day seemed to recharge their batteries. The tradition of keeping the Sabbath (be it Friday, Saturday or Sunday) as a day of rest appears to be good for us physically and psychologically – not just spiritually. Countries who have abandoned the weekly day of rest may well find the cost to health and happiness very high.

The rhythms of life

Working *with* your natural body rhythms rather than against them will help you to achieve a better balance in your life: a balance between adequate sleep, rest, stimulation and pure pleasure (both physical and emotional).

The circadian rhythm. Many people quite naturally use this body rhythm (which occurs or recurs once each day) to set their sleep time consistently each day. Others are able to sleep any time in spite of the rhythm; they can easily switch off. Still others can have disturbances in their circadian rhythm (for example one of twenty-five hours instead of twenty-four hours), which can dramatically interfere with sleep. As mentioned earlier, this also happens with jet lag and with shift workers.

To keep your inner clock running on time, make sure you wake and *get up* at the same time each day (even on weekends and holidays) and either go outside or go into very bright light. The light falling through your eyes onto the pineal gland sets your internal clock and helps keep the circadian rhythm regular and accurate. This will make your going-to-sleep time more predictable and regular.

The ultradian rhythm. The 1½–2-hour ultradian rhythm that occurs during the day and night can be used to optimise the time at which you go to bed. At the beginning of this cycle there is a short 'window' (about

10–15 minutes) of time in which you will more easily fall asleep.

To calculate this time take note, firstly after lunch and then later in the afternoon, of the times at which you notice either drowsiness, loss of concentration, daydreaming, unexplained sexual arousal or sudden driving fatigue occurring. The elapsed time between two such events gives you the length of your cycle. Then count forward to the time you need to be going to bed to wait for your 'window' of sleep. For instance, if you first noticed drowsiness at 2 p.m. and then again at 3.45 p.m., your cycle would be one hour forty-five minutes. Counting forward from 3.45 p.m., you would expect to be ready for sleep at 9 p.m. or 10.45 p.m.

If you go to bed and don't go to sleep within half an hour, get up and go to another room to do relaxing activities for an hour until the next 'window' approaches.

It is easier to identify your ultradian cycle and its period on a day that is not too demanding and on which you are not overdosing on caffeine.

Sleep rituals

If you get into a routine or you ritualise the things you do every night (for example you put the cat out, lock doors, clean teeth, shower, and go to bed), your mind and body learn to trigger sleep as you do these tasks.

If you are still having difficulties, seek professional advice. Remember, however, that it is most important to keep the problem in perspective and do some accurate diary-keeping, with your partner making observations as well. This helps identify more easily the real factors involved. But if you suspect you have sleep apnoea or narcolepsy, do not delay in seeking medical help.

Staying happy

You don't necessarily have to be healthy to be happy and there are plenty of happy people who drink too much, eat too much and smoke. But there is a strong connection between being healthy and being happy that can't be ignored. Happier people tend to be healthier even if they do smoke, over-imbibe alcoholic refreshments and have diets that seem to break all the rules. Happiness and personality can also influence the triggering of illness and its prognosis.

> *There is a strong connection between being healthy and being happy that can't be ignored.*

In recognition of the associations between your emotional state and your physical state, the *Diagnostic and Statistical Annual of Mental Diseases* (basically a handbook for diagnosis used by psychologists and psychiatrists) now includes a category called 'psychological factors affecting medical condition'. The area of science that studies these connections is called psychoneuroimmunology and psychoneuroendocrinology — basically the mindbody connection.

If a person is so unhappy that they are depressed, this will significantly affect the course of conditions such as psoriasis and acne, and illnesses such as cardiovascular disease, stroke, multiple sclerosis, Parkinson's disease and epilepsy. Depression will also affect the prognosis and chances of survival of those suffering myocardial infarction, renal disease, and certain cancers (particularly breast cancer and melanoma). People with rheumatoid arthritis suffer more pain and have longer acute episodes with less satisfactory recovery and rehabilitation if they are depressed.

Anxiety can particularly exacerbate irritable bowel syndrome, oesophageal motility disorders, peptic ulcers and Crohn's disease, severe acne and asthma. Leading researchers in the area of personality style and illness claim they can predict with 80-per-cent accuracy whether healthy people will develop cancer or heart disease — depending on personality. People who have a personality style that is angry and hostile (as opposed to experiencing occasional outbursts) seem to be more prone to developing atherosclerosis and cardiac arrhythmias. This is thought to be because an angry, hostile attitude leads to chronic actuation of stress hormones, which increase the deposition of plaque on the lining of blood vessels and cause changes in heart rhythm. People more likely to get cancer tend to be highly rational peacemakers who suppress their emotions and deny their feelings. Personality factors have also been associated with cancer of the cervix and uterus.

The physical effect of acute or chronic stress can cause and exacerbate eczema, atopic dermatitis and pruritus. Unresolved physical or emotional trauma can also influence health; however, you do not have to discover, remember or re-experience trauma in order to resolve it. In fact, this can be counter-productive and even dangerous. To safely resolve things that you suspect are influencing your health, see a psychologist trained to treat the effects of trauma.

There is now overwhelming evidence that emotional and psychological factors play a crucial role in the development, cause and prognosis of an illness.

Of course, what this is telling us is that our feelings are crucial to our health. If you think back to the 'chain reaction', feelings come from our self-talk, which is determined by our beliefs, which evolve from our perceptions. So if we want to be healthier, we need to look not only at the lifestyle factors mentioned earlier, but also at what's going on in our minds.

> *If we want to be healthier, we need to look not only at lifestyle factors, but also at what's going on in our minds.*

Believing you can be healthy

From the time we are very young our family's attitudes about health and ill health shape our own beliefs about being healthy and getting sick. The absence of easy access to professional medical help for earlier genera-tions meant that people's general attitude to illness was mostly one of self-reliance. If you got a serious illness, you probably died anyway.

But with the advent of better hygiene, the decrease in many infectious killers, and the lower morbidity in childbirth, people generally believe that if they are sick the doctor and a pill will cure them, rather than believing in their own responsibility to stay healthy in the first place. It is only very recently, with the blow-out in health budgets throughout the Western world, that a shift is occurring to try to put responsibility for the maintenance of health back onto individuals.

This is a long, slow process that is meeting strong resistance from a population that has been encouraged to hand over responsibility for their health to others. However, the alarming rise in iatrogenic illness (illness caused by the treatment of some other illness, usually a drug reaction or surgical complication), and the fact that the billions spent on pharmaceuticals have lengthened lives rather than made them healthier, has forced a change in attitude to how we maintain health and treat disease. Iatrogenic illness has been estimated in Western medicine to occupy about 60 per cent of all hospital admission days and account for about 30 per cent of all illnesses. So it makes good sense for individuals to start believing that they should try to stay healthy.

Your family's beliefs about illness also influence whether you believe health or illness is the norm.

> Your family's beliefs about illness also influence whether you believe health or illness is the norm.

Depressed or anxious parents can be constantly visiting conventional or alternative health practitioners in an attempt to relieve physical symptoms that have basically emotional causes. Occasionally when I have lectured about stress to students, even primary students, I have asked them to tell me who has visited a doctor or naturopath in the last month. It is not unusual to have at least a third of the children raise their hands. When asked if anybody in the family has visited a health practitioner of any kind in the last month, over 80 per cent have put up their hands. To these children and many adults the belief is that blooming health is an abnormal condition!

One large study showed that people's beliefs about their health were a better predictor of morbidity than an objective assessment by their doctor. Those who believed their health was OK, regardless of the reality, lived longer than those who believed that their health was not OK, even when according to their doctors they were actually 'healthier'.

So if you want to start being healthy, have a good look at whether you believe health is normal, and at whether you think you *can* and *deserve to* be healthy.

Stress can be good for you

If you believe that all stress in your life is bad and can adversely affect your health, your consequent self-talk and the chain reaction that follows is not going to help your feelings, your behaviour or your health.

Stress is your reaction to emotional or physical changes in your life. But changes can be good or bad. Getting married may be the best thing that ever happened to you, but it also demands many adjustments and changes to your normal routine. Good stressors in your life are called eu-stress whereas the negative stressors in your life are called dis-stress. If you had no stress in your life you would be very bored, and in fact the under-stimulation could be stressful in itself.

> ℞ Stress is your reaction to emotional or physical changes in your life. But changes can be good or bad. If you had no stress in your life you would be very bored, and in fact under-stimulation could be stressful in itself. ℞

Too little stress or too few demands means our performance is sub-optimal. Too much stress in the form of too many demands leads to low performance as well. Athletes talk about being 'in the zone', where the demands and level of stress they create in their bodies is at optimal level for peak performance. The same can happen with our everyday lives. When the demands being made on us (or those we make on ourselves) are greater than our ability to meet them, we feel stressed. It's important to believe and understand that not all stress is bad and that eu-stress can make us happy and healthy. Whether we feel dis-tressed or eu-stressed depends greatly on the meaning we attach to the demands; that is, our self-talk about the situation.

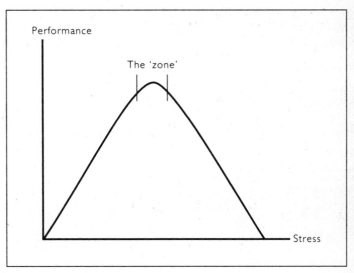

Stress and performance

Crying is good for you

Unfortunately, many cultures place a premium on not expressing emotions, and Western macho cultures tend to discourage boys in particular from crying. Fortunately, this is beginning to change because crying appears to be very good for you physically as well as emotionally. Apart from anecdotal reports that asthma attacks have ceased when people allow themselves to

> ℞ Crying is an important eliminative process for the chemicals that would otherwise build up in the body due to stress. ℞

cry more, recent studies have shown that the chemical composition of tears varies according to the circumstances. Emotional tears are different from laughter tears, which are different from tears caused by irritants like peeling onions.

It's beginning to look as though crying is an important eliminative process for the chemicals that would otherwise build up in the body due to stress. If you feel upset, there are ways to get your tears to flow, for example by watching a sad video, thinking about a sad event, reading a moving passage in a novel, or listening to evocative music. Using appropriate acu-pressure points or deep breathing can also be helpful. You can literally feel a lot 'cleaner' and lighter inside when you have had a good cry.

Can the mind cure the body?

Placebos are a fascinating phenomenon that illustrates how the mind and body influence each other. A placebo is anything – a substance, a ritual, a behaviour – that a patient believes will relieve their symptoms or even induce symptoms. In some studies the placebo effect has been found to be as high as 60 per cent, while an average of 30 per cent of people attributed significant symptom relief to a placebo. The more powerful the belief, the stronger a placebo's effect is likely to be.

Consider how few treatment options medical practitioners had to offer their patients in the past. That they continued to be consulted, and that many patients got well, suggests that much of what was happening was being determined by the self-healing mechanisms of their own mindbody.

Despite a rich and profound knowledge of herbal medicines, medicine men of indigenous cultures rely a great deal on 'magic' and rituals — promoting the patient's belief in their magical healing powers. Australian Aboriginal healers have told me that much of what they do is triggering self-healing processes.

Placebos can even counter the effect of drugs and create an opposite effect. In one case, a woman suffering continual nausea and vomiting that had resisted all previous medication was told that she was to be given a new experimental drug. In fact, the medication was a syrup of ipecac, normally given to induce vomiting. Within twenty minutes her nausea and vomiting had stopped and her stomach motility returned to normal. This case illustrates not just the importance of belief in a placebo but the expectation of the outcome as well.

Sometimes people come to consult me from interstate and overseas. Some of these patients stand out because a single consultation has caused such dramatic changes and improvement in symptoms. The normal expectation effects that operate in all medical and psychological treatment are heightened in these people because the patient has often gone to extreme lengths to track me down. From the time they started their search the powerful self-healing effects of their own body had become mobilised, so by the time I saw them they were well primed to get maximum benefit from anything I said or did. Every parent is familiar with making an urgent appointment to take a child to the doctor only to find they make a miraculous recovery as soon as they know they are going.

HARRY, TOM AND PENNY – A CASE STUDY

One day a man called Harry rang from Broome in the top north-west corner of Australia to speak to me in the bottom south-east corner of the country. He couldn't have been further away, with several deserts and many thousands of kilometres between us. He had recently been given custody of two children: a niece of eight (Penny) and a nephew of ten (Tom), whose parents had been killed in a car accident. The children's parents had had difficult, unsettled lives and the children were somewhat 'wild'. Harry's own life had been rather eventful, but the responsibility of these two children had focused his life dramatically. He had stopped 'hitting the bottle' and didn't smoke indoors any more because of his niece's asthma.

On the phone he sounded a real rough diamond and I enjoyed getting to know him. His problem was that not only had the children missed a lot of school and fallen seriously behind academically, but he'd noticed that their behaviour seemed always 'jumpy'. They couldn't keep still, they had night sweats, frequent diarrhoea, night terrors, rashes and a whole host of other behavioural and physical symptoms. Although Harry had never been the slightest bit interested in his own or anybody else's health, it didn't make sense to him that the doctor said the children were healthy when they had all these distressing symptoms. A magazine review of my first book, which explored the connections between health, emotional problems and foods and chemicals, had set him thinking.

Since there were so many social problems in Harry's and the children's past and present circumstances, I was very concerned when Harry announced that he was travelling across Australia for me to 'fix the kids'. No matter what I said or offered to do by working with the community and school resources he had in Broome, he was adamant that I could fix them.

For the next six months I would get regular phone calls from Harry as he drove slowly across Australia in an old station wagon, which became his and the children's home. The vehicle broke down constantly and often he'd stop for a week or two and work to get money to continue the journey.

Harry followed the guidelines from my book regarding a sensible diet and so on, and his calls always entailed questions about handling the kids as well. He was a quick learner with a great intuitive understanding of children, even though he had had virtually nothing to do with them previously and he was fifty years of age.

Eventually the car broke down completely and they then started catching a series of buses. Sometimes Harry would put me on the line to 'tell the kids what they had to do to get better'. The children were in awe of this god that Harry had created and they could say little but 'yes' or 'no' in hushed voices.

Finally they arrived. Harry had insisted they splurge and stay at a local caravan park the night before they saw me, and when they came they were all scrubbed until their faces shone. Harry apologised for their crumpled appearance, explaining that the iron at the caravan park didn't work!

I really liked Harry. His broken teeth and his limp (from

a rodeo accident) gave a glimpse of what must have been a very hard life.

Harry reported that the children had already improved dramatically. He attributed this to living mostly on bush tucker and having almost no sugar; however, the little girl's eczema was still a problem and the boy was still 'too moody' according to Harry.

The journey had brought this wonderful man very close to these children whom he hadn't even known until a few months ago, and it was touching to see how gentle and caring such a rough diamond could be with them.

I noticed that Tom had many warts over his hands which he rubbed constantly. Harry reported that the doctor had given up trying to treat them. I ignored the moody symptoms, which I suspected from all that Harry had told me on the journey had a lot to do with his grief for his parents. I focused on the warts, telling Tom that as each day went by and his body needed more and more energy to grow, the warts would get less and less nourishment, and would wither and die and eventually fall off. I also suggested that as he grew he would find it easier to talk about and deal with things that upset him, and this would make him feel better inside. It was only a matter of waiting while his body grew. I could see from Tom's clothes that he was probably having a growth spurt, so he readily accepted this.

Penny's eczema was almost gone but her constant scratching was really stopping the natural healing of her skin. I told her that her skin hadn't quite learnt yet that the eczema was actually better and didn't need to itch any more, and that with each day as her skin forgot it had eczema, it would also forget to be itchy.

Harry himself talked and talked and I said almost nothing. He desperately needed reassurance that he was the best person to take care of Tom and Penny – not foster parents – and that he could be a successful parent.

As the nearest bus stop was some distance from my rooms I drove them there and waved them goodbye, feeling the world needed more people with Harry's commitment.

A fortnight later he rang, thrilled to say that Tom's warts were already going, that he was talking to Harry far more, and that he was less moody and seemed generally happier in himself. Penny had stopped scratching almost immediately, and her legs were nearly healed. They were going back to Broome although he thought it might 'take a while' as he had to earn the funds to do so.

Eighteen months later I received a photograph of a smiling Harry with his arms around a grinning Tom and Penny, who had just completed the first full year of school in their lives.

I'm sure that the transformation in Harry, Tom and Penny was due not so much to that one visit, but to the expectation they had that everything would be better once they had put in all that effort to help themselves.

Self-talk to make you better

Our beliefs influence what we feel about health and disease. Whether we feel dis-tressed or eu-stressed depends on the meaning that we attach to what happens to us.

A study of soldiers wounded during the Second World War showed that only a quarter needed strong medication for severe injuries which, if suffered by civilians in an accident, all would have required very strong medication. Many doctors have noticed in other war zones that the soldiers who complain of the most pain have the least serious injuries. However, for soldiers compared to civilians, and for soldiers with minor injuries compared to those with serious injuries, the meaning is quite different. For a civilian, injury can mean loss of income, damage to property such as a car, disruption to daily life, threat to employment and so on, but for a soldier severe injury means a ticket home and no more war. A soldier with a minor injury will recover and be sent back to the war zone, whereas one with a serious injury goes home.

> 🖎 *The meaning you attach to illnesses will affect how sick you feel and can influence the length of your recovery and ultimate prognosis.* 🖎

In everyday life the meaning you attach to illnesses will also affect how sick you feel and can influence the length of your recovery and ultimate prognosis. When a cancer patient is told that over 50 per cent of cancer patients will die of something other than cancer, their attitude towards their cancer changes dramatically. Similarly if you say 50 per cent of patients will live rather than 50 per cent will die, you will feel very differently about your chances in surgery.

BILL AND SAM – A CASE STUDY

Some years ago I was working in rehabilitation. In one ward there were two young men, Bill and Sam, who were of the same age and who had both lost their right legs above the knee in motorbike accidents. Their other injuries were relatively minor.

Within days of surgery Bill was practising with a temporary prosthesis and he 'walked' out of hospital within four weeks. Bill was a bricklayer, who stood all day on scaffolding. He very quickly accepted his injury and started to think of ways to make bricklaying easier as well as to work out how he could still go skiing next winter.

Sam, a computer programmer, was extremely distressed. His stump took months to heal properly. He complained constantly of the rubbing and discomfort of his prosthesis and he was repeatedly re-admitted to hospital with every imaginable complication. Even though to an observer the loss of his leg would have less impact on his life than on that of the bricklayer, the meaning that Sam gave to losing his leg had a far more devastating effect that created intolerable anguish for him.

Healthy people tend to cope better with the stressors of life and those that cope better stay healthier. If you believe that no matter what happens you will find the strength and resources – either from within yourself or from those around you – to deal with the situation, you will cope better and suffer less. Not liking or wanting a situation is different from not being able to cope with it.

Those that suffer least stress are the people who can accept what has happened and get on with dealing with it. Their energy is focused on tackling the problem rather than on fighting it. Once you can accept a situation, the anguish begins to dissipate.

Your style of self-talk can even affect your immune system. If you lose someone close to you, your immune system can be impaired. The better your self-talk style for dealing with major loss such as bereavement, the faster your immune system returns to normal. Indeed, in studies of coping styles, those that coped well with stressful events had better natural killer cell activity (NKCA) in their immune systems than poor copers.

Your style of self-talk also affects your expectations of yourself and how you assess your performance. In a study of glandular fever in a group of cadets at a military academy, it was found that although a fifth of the year's intake of cadets became infected (as shown in blood tests), only a quarter of them actually developed symptoms. Those that did develop symptoms were not achieving as highly as they or their fathers expected. Their lower-than-expected results appear to have directly affected their immune system and their susceptibility to infection.

How much your coping style can influence an illness once you have it is still contentious. However, it does seem very clear that your coping style, and in particular your style of self-talk, can greatly improve your resistance to disease generally. There is also evidence that being able to see the funny side of things and to laugh affects not only your immune function, but also how happy and healthy you feel — even in the face of devastating illness.

One of the people who made the most impression

on me when I was a child was a family friend who was extraordinarily full of life and fun. Even as I watched her very slowly die of breast cancer I marvelled at how she could always see the funny side of a situation. One day Jo commented that as she removed her wig, teeth, and false boobs and put them away in a drawer before going to bed the night before, she had suggested that her husband might be better off in the drawer than with what was left of her in bed! She kept this delicious sense of humour right to the end of her life. As an adult, I've sometimes wondered to what extent her determination to see the funny side had also been a way of denying her real feelings. A little bit of denial can actually be very healthy and helpful. But when it stops you from allowing yourself to have any negative feelings, it can undermine your immune system and your health quite badly. Breast cancer patients who get angry and hostile, and are described as 'difficult' by their doctors, live longest. Those who stay 'lovely people', are passive and 'nice', seem to die sooner.

Watching humour provides great stress relief and a boost to your immune system, and seeing the funny side of life instead of the tragic can be an essential survival technique for anyone with emotionally intense jobs in the police force, social work or medical professions, and the like. To outsiders, the humour of these people can seem inappropriate, but to them it can mean the difference between functioning effectively and burning out – fast.

Even if you don't work in an emotionally charged or heartrending job, a good sense of humour that doesn't take life too seriously is an enormous asset.

Just using the words and imagery of fun and humour can help. For instance, compare your feelings when you describe teenage boys as 'impossibly noisy, clumsy and contrary' with your feelings when you describe them as 'a bunch of irrepressible half-grown, undisciplined puppies'. The first description makes you feel annoyed and irritated; the second can bring a smile to your face.

Lighten up. Let yourself enjoy the funny side of life.

Feelings

If you take control of your self-talk about illness, you also take greater control of your feelings. If a woman

> If you take control of your self-talk about illness, you also take greater control of your feelings.

believes that menstruation is a woman's curse, she will be more likely to have 'difficult' periods. If a woman feels menopause inevitably creates health problems for women, she will be more likely to have bothersome menopausal symptoms. A man worried about premature ejaculation will be more likely to have this problem.

MABEL – A CASE STUDY

If you have a chronic condition you can still *feel* healthy!

One delightful woman called Mabel came to see me. She had been diagnosed with progressive multiple sclerosis some years previously. She was in a wheelchair, her vision was affected and she was becoming increasingly dependent on her family. Yet she still had a very wide circle of friends and interests and had just started a computer course to give her greater communication and access to resources. She came to see me, keen to learn ideodynamic healing techniques.

After giving me her history, which apart from the MS included many sad and tragic events in her life, she suddenly stopped talking and said, 'Look, don't get the wrong impression, I'm actually very healthy'.

I've seen many patients like Mabel who, despite having even very serious illnesses, feel well, and see themselves as healthy people with a particular condition rather than as people who are sick. Feeling well can be as much, if not more, determined by your self-talk than by what's actually wrong with you. As mentioned earlier, how people describe their own health is a better predictor of their life expectancy than an objective health assessment by a doctor! As long as

you believe your health is good, the professional's opinion doesn't necessarily mean much.

The experience and management of pain depends not just on the meaning of the pain discussed earlier but also on how much control you feel you have over the pain. When patients are taught pain management skills, the pacing of activities is an important component. If a person has an injured shoulder, three hours of continuous ironing or working on an assembly line will be hell. But the more the person is shown how to pace and change activities to meet their needs, the less pain they will suffer and the less disabled they will see themselves. Similarly, arthritis patients who are taught pacing skills can achieve just as much as, if not more than, untrained patients, but with considerably less pain.

In a revealing experiment, soldiers were told they were going on a long march, and their experience of stress was measured in terms of cortisol and proactin levels. The amount of distress reported and measured was dramatically different, depending on what they were told about how far they were going, how realistic the reports of progress were or whether they were given any reports at all. Those kept fully and accurately informed of the distance and progress suffered far less stress than those given no details or misleading information. How they felt was determined by what went on in their heads and this affected the level of psychological stress they suffered.

Acknowledging and expressing strong feelings about experiences and traumas by writing about them has been found to improve immunity to disease. One group of university students was asked to write about their daily activities over four days. Another group wrote about their innermost feelings and seriously upsetting events in their lives. At the end of four days, both groups were given hepatitis B vaccinations. Those who had written about their deeper feelings developed significantly higher levels of antibodies against hepatitis B than those who just recorded their daily life. The greatest immune response was found in the students who had written about the more serious experiences.

You don't have to be afraid of unhappiness or uncontrolled feelings. Rather you need to realise how useful they can be.

> ✎ *You don't have to be afraid of unhappiness or uncontrolled feelings. Rather you need to realise how useful they can be.* ✎

At first glance the following feelings may seem destructive and to be avoided at all costs:

- anxiety
- stress
- fear
- anger
- confusion
- defeat
- depression
- emptiness
- frustration
- grief
- guilt
- insecurity
- isolation
- loneliness
- misery
- pressure
- worry
- weepiness.

But before you run away from those feelings by breaking relationships, changing jobs or abusing drugs, stop and ask yourself where the feelings are coming from. If you allow them to, negative feelings can act as constructive triggers to get you to:

- stop
- re-assess the situation
- change your thinking and your behaviour
- act in a way that is more constructive.

Discomfort is a message telling you something is wrong in your life or with your way of handling things that happen. If you blindly run away from discomfort, you can never feel contentment or peace

> ꙮ *Discomfort is a message telling you something is wrong in your life or with your way of handling things that happen.* ꙮ

of mind because you never confront what is going wrong.

Sometimes, of course, the best thing to do is to run as fast as you can! But learn to realise that you can deal with discomfort, if not by yourself then with appropriate help.

Remember to ask yourself 'What is my discomfort trying to tell me?'

Behaviour

You will be healthier if you behave as healthy people do. Those people who work (despite illness), who socialise (despite illness), who are involved with family

Discomfort is a message telling you something is wrong in your life

life and who are needed by others (despite illness) stay healthier longer – even if their level of activity is severely limited.

Focusing on what you can do rather than on what you can't do, and doing it, keeps you healthier. Brett Nielson, in Australia's first case of disability caused by thalidomide, was born without arms. And yet as he put it, 'This is me. I'm not a tragic figure ... I have the best life of anyone I know ... Thalidomide is not really a key factor in my life'. Brett runs a highly successful recording studio, has a family, and lives on an acreage that he looks after himself. He's learnt to manipulate his feet and toes the way other people use their hands and fingers.

> ☙ *Focusing on what you can do rather than what you can't do, and doing it, keeps you healthier.* ☙

Research has consistently shown that once the shock of major illness or trauma has gone and a person readjusts their self-image, they can still be very happy and see themselves as healthy.

In short ...

☙ Feel good and look good; look good and feel good.

☙ If you want to be healthy, do what healthy people do.

☙ Check on this before you think about losing weight: are you using food for comfort? Maybe you need to sort out a few things that have nothing to do with food.

❧ Whether exercise helps for psychological or physiological reasons is not clear, nor is it important – just do it.

❧ Balance work and leisure, activity and rest.

❧ Work with your natural body rhythms to get adequate good-quality rest.

❧ Don't underestimate the links between happiness and health.

❧ Believe that you can be healthy and that you have the right to be so.

❧ Have a good cry if you feel like it.

❧ Self-talk influences your health: faith-healing is not just a myth.

The 7th Secret: Healthy people are socially connected

The 'glue' that binds us

Humans are social animals.

Our need for each other goes way beyond the need for a mate to reproduce and to support child rearing. In their book *The Healing Brain* Robert Ornstein and David Sobel review intriguing research into the crucial role that the degree of our 'social connectedness' plays in keeping us healthy, happy and sane. Some research has found that if people are single, separated, divorced or widowed, they are five to ten times more likely to be hospitalised for a mental illness or emotional problem and two or three times more likely to die than if they are married. General resistance to all diseases appears to be greatly influenced by how well and how satisfyingly people are socially supported. It would also seem that simply having a strong sense of commitment to another, even in what could be

seen as a 'bad' marriage, is an important factor.

Your health does not begin and end with you as an individual but is clearly dependent on what is happening in your emotional as well as your physical environment.

This has been well recognised in indigenous cultures. For tens of thousands of years the Australian Aboriginal medicine men have known that treatment sometimes means ignoring the patient while first checking what has been happening with the patient's spouse, extended family and neighbouring tribes, as well as what has been happening with their physical environment. Treatment can have more to do with telling the family to behave themselves than with focusing on the symptoms of the patient.

A number of studies have confirmed that the degree of social cohesion (defined as the degree of stability within the social group) is one of the crucial factors in the emotional and physical wellbeing of people.

> Your health is clearly dependent on what is happening in your emotional as well as your physical environment.

Consequently, the more socially cohesive the group, the lower the incidence of suicide. While the suicide rate increases in times of great social change, boom times, recessions and wars, it is still far less in the most socially cohesive groups. Widows involved in one or more community groups and with relatives living close by are less likely to become suicidal than those widows who are relatively isolated within their communities.

How well supported you are in the community also affects your attitude to seeking medical advice when you need it and following through with diagnostic and treatment procedures. The area in which I live is geographically isolated from big city treatment centres, especially for radiotherapy and chemotherapy. It has a high proportion of retirees who have moved away from their families and old social networks. If they need treatment for cancer, many find the daily 200-kilometre round trip, plus hours of waiting at the hospital, too arduous and choose to forgo

> ❧ How well supported you are in the community affects your attitude to seeking medical advice when you need it. ❧

treatment. However, those with spouses prepared to drive them or a network of friends prepared to help can pursue even repeated rounds of treatment.

One study showed that if you live alone for whatever reason, you need to be involved in at least three other social networks to compensate for the health benefits of living with people. These networks may be related to work, sport or a hobby, but they need to engage you in satisfying activities where your contribution to the group is as important as what you get out of it. There is a need to be needed.

Perhaps what is most startling about the emerging research into social factors and health is the degree to which social connectedness can override other known and more traditionally accepted risk factors such as smoking, alcohol consumption, amount of exercise, diet and obesity. It would seem that being socially isolated and disconnected increases your susceptibility to disease generally, although there are plenty of people who still get sick and die despite loving families and important community roles.

Early studies into the differences in longevity between Japanese people living in Japan, Hawaii and California attributed the higher rate of heart disease and cancer the greater distance they moved away from Japan to changes in diet. However, later more detailed studies also looked at the social relationships of Japanese in Japan, Hawaii and California. These studies found that Japanese expatriates who maintained the same kind of social and family networking in Hawaii and California as they did in Japan had the same longevity despite the changes in diet causing high serum cholesterol, bad smoking habits and high blood pressure similar to the local Western population. Social connectedness and social cohesion appears to protect these people in the face of known health risk factors.

This greater importance of social connectedness over known risk factors has also been shown in retrenched workers, pregnant women and a number of different social and religious groups.

Even owning a pet or caring for plants can provide protective health benefits fulfilling that need to be needed. Animals that strongly interact with humans, such as dogs, cats, monkeys and horses, provide the bonus of unqualified acceptance of yourself that is sadly lacking in other relationships. But even a tortoise or a fish will do! Heart attack victims with pets had five times the survival rate, after twelve months, those without pets. Even watching a goldfish or stroking a pet will lower blood pressure.

> ꙮ *Heart attack victims with pets had five times the survival rate, after twelve months, of those without pets.* ꙮ

However, the more committed you are to your pet and the more directly responsible you are for its wellbeing, the greater the benefits. Remember the patients in the nursing home with their pot plants (see page 95).

From an evolutionary point of view, the ability to form extremely strong social attachments has been vital in humans because the human baby's brain develops mostly after birth. The social environment of our children is infinitely more important to their development than it is for other animals, hence the need for very strong emotional attachments to support lengthy and ongoing social networks of co-operation.

The alarming consequences to our health when strong emotional attachments are broken has been revealed in studies of people who have recently lost a spouse due to illness or trauma. These bereavement studies showed measurable depression of the immune system after such a loss, which lasted many months. The immune system returned to normal as people grieved and adjusted to their loss.

This depression of the immune system would help explain the increased incidence of infections, general ill health and even cancer in people during the two years following the death of a spouse. The illnesses can be severe or minor: allergies, digestive disturbances, rashes and a lengthening of the healing time for cuts, abrasions and burns.

> ☙ The social environment of our children is infinitely more important to their development than it is for other animals, hence the need for very strong emotional attachments. ☙

Even hostile arguments between people married for a very long time can quite dramatically increase the production of stress hormones, which then lower resistance to disease. One study showed women to be much more affected by hostile arguments and for much longer after the argument than men. The longer a couple had been together, the greater the effect. Couples did not get used to rows, but became more sensitive with age.

One aspect of social connectedness that has received little attention, but which acts like glue to give communities a sense of cohesion and common purpose, is the common ownership of important social assets:

public hospitals, roads, water supply, power and energy sources, communications, public transport, parks and gardens, national parks, reserves, municipal offices, theatres, halls and recreational facilities.

Because of the extraordinary zeal shown by economists for privatisation and competition, the latter have been likened to new fundamentalist religions. Unfortunately this zeal has led to a staggering social experiment in England, New Zealand and Australia, based on assumptions about human beings

'Privatising the air has been the most profitable deal yet'

that have no scientific basis and which actually go against what we do know about human behaviour.

The Americans already had a highly individualistic society, which has now become so determined to protect individual rights (such as gun ownership, and freedom of speech) that it impinges on the rights of others (the right to live safely, the right not to be racially or religiously vilified).

We know that in order to be healthy and happy people, we need to be useful members of a social structure working co-operatively together, not just for the good of the individual but for the good of the community as a whole. Optimum health and happiness comes from a balance between a respect for individual needs, community needs and the need for individuals to be involved in something bigger than themselves. Too much emphasis placed on the good of the group at the expense of the individual leads to

> *In order to be healthy and happy people, we need to be useful members of a social structure working co-operatively together.*

a decrease in personal happiness. If the individual's needs are severely compromised, health also suffers.

Co-operation, not competition

Competition between human beings does not continuously improve performance; in many cases competition destroys effectiveness.

Setting one employee or work team against another in competition became the corporate fashion throughout the late 1970s and the 1980s. However, the corporate world quickly discovered that short-term gains masked serious long-term problems. The 'compete at all costs' philosophy also implies there will be winners and losers in this competition. If the competition is *between* businesses, that can be (but is not automatically) a good thing. When you use the same philosophy, however, to pit one employee against another, especially with secret individual contracts and deals, then you no longer have an organisation working together for a common cause. Instead you have a bunch of individuals who are constantly watching their backs, becoming highly protective of information and ideas to give them an edge over others.

Some businesses realised fairly quickly where this obsession with individual competition was leading, and in the corporate world co-operation, negotiation and teamwork are now the buzz words. It is as if they have suddenly discovered something of which human beings have previously been ignorant. It may be news to accountants and economists but ordinary people and the social sciences have always known this rather basic truth.

Unfortunately, just as the corporate world was discovering the messy and destructive consequences of ferocious individual competition, governments and their advisers found the faith and started ripping up the fabric of the government and public service operations in order to introduce this magical component called efficiency. 'Efficiency comes through competition and privatisation' has become the chant of the devoted in governments across much of the Western world (although Europeans seem to have been more prudent) despite research that clearly shows that the opposite can be true.

If the effects of pitting one employee against another in an organisation can be disastrous for business, they can be cataclysmic in organisations that are supposed to put the public and their needs first, for example education, medicine, telecommunications, public transport, roads, power and water supply. Employees no longer work co-operatively to meet the needs of the public either in the short term or in the long term. Instead they must focus on out-performing other employees and meeting the performance targets of their own contracts. Worse problems for the public develop when these performance targets are based only on the short-term values of accountants and economists rather than on those of ordinary people and professionals in social science who are trained to look at outcomes for individuals and long-term social consequences.

In education, the placing of teachers on secret contracts with their principals creates an appalling climate of suspicion and distrust. Volunteers sitting on councils and sub-committees have no knowledge of whether the idea being pushed is for sound educational purposes or because that person will get a handsome bonus for pushing it through. In this climate not only do staff pull back their effort to prevent their being manipulated and used, but so too do parents and volunteers.

In organisations such as schools and hospitals trusting, collaborative teamwork between staff, community, students and parents is crucial for the best human outcome. Social connectedness depends on co-operation and trust leading to intimate bonding. This is impossible in the atmosphere of secrecy and 'me first' created by the obsession with competition. Social connectedness also means feeling

Community ownership of assets gives an essential feeling of shared responsibility and commitment to other people.

a sense of belonging to the larger community. This has been maintained throughout human existence by the community's shared ownership of important assets basic to its survival: water, land, and later public infrastructure such as roads, transport, energy sources, and so on. This community ownership of assets gives an essential feeling of shared responsibility and commitment to other people and to future generations. The 'user pays' approach, when taken to extremes, takes away this feeling of mutual responsibility and need of each other.

As a child I lived in the country, and a train or tram ride when we visited the city was an exciting experience. I'd often thought it would be nice to own my own train or tram, and one day I mentioned this to my mother. To my amazement she said, 'But you do!' She went on to explain how we all paid taxes and that, as well as the fares, this paid for us to own trams, trains, roads, dams, art galleries, and so on. For a while one of my favourite pastimes was asking my parents if we all owned this, that and whatever: the beach, the sky, the park, the footpaths, the frogs, the birds ... I'll never forget the pride, power and sense of belonging it gave me to realise that I was part of a group that shared all that! Sitting on a train had new meaning; the other passengers were suddenly no longer strangers but joint owners in this wonderful venture called a railway.

My childhood discovery and my delight in belonging to a community is no different from what we know all people need in order to be healthier and happier: the feeling of social connectedness where individual needs and freedoms are balanced with the needs of the group, and where the glue that keeps us together is shared responsibility, commitment and ownership of community assets.

When responsibility for prisoners, the disadvantaged, the sick, and the unemployed is off-loaded to 'private providers', the onus of responsibility and accountability is shifted from the community itself through its government to external agents. This sends a subtle but strong message that the government and therefore the community does not want to be bothered with people who cannot look after themselves. For instance, handing over responsibility for prisons to others makes it easier for the community to abdicate responsibility for social conditions that can exacerbate or create crime.

Of course, to own and maintain community services requires adequate taxation. There is nothing wrong with demanding value for money and the efficient use of public funds, but the cry for lower and lower levels of taxation at some point means services go. Usually those in a community with the least power – women, children and the poor – suffer as a consequence.

Reducing taxes throws more responsibility onto individuals to provide for themselves: health care, education, disability services, and so on. This breeds resentment in those people struggling on their own towards people and groups receiving any form of public support.

Paying taxes really means being prepared to share, to care about other people and to value belonging to a large, socially cohesive group, which we know is crucial to health and happiness. The myth circulated by economists that public ownership precludes efficiency and cost-effectiveness is slowly being exploded, even by other economists. The challenge is not to dissolve the social glue but rather to look at its weaknesses and to strengthen it.

> ✒ *The challenge is not to dissolve the social glue but to look at its weaknesses and strengthen it.* ✒

Social cohesion

Health and happiness are dependent on living in a stable, harmonious and secure community, but maintaining social cohesion, particularly in multicultural communities, is no easy matter.

If we demand individualism from people we tend to isolate them, making them insecure, fearful and more self-centered in order to survive. Unfortunately, when people feel threatened they become less tolerant of differences and look for scapegoats. The existence of scapegoats stops people feeling overwhelmed by the thought that they are totally responsible for their predicament.

This situation can become very dangerous. The need to feel connected to a group remains, and if government policy is in effect telling people they are on their own and can no longer rely on the community, people will band together in smaller, often ethnic or common-interest groups such as cults and lobby groups, instead. Because members feel threatened, these groups can in turn develop their own siege mentality, further isolating sub-groups from mainstream society.

But a community that encourages or allows passive dependency doesn't promote health and happiness either as it robs people of a sense of personal control. Achieving a balance between shared community responsibility and individual responsibility is not easy; but to do so we have to consider the solid research of the social and behavioural sciences, not just dubious and shaky economic theories and fashions.

To enable people from diverse value systems to feel equally part of their wider community, there need to be deliberate policies to achieve social cohesion. In a cohesive, modern, democratic society, *every* individual has to feel that they matter and that what they think matters equally. At the same time there has to be a shared value system that acts as a common denominator and that welds the community together in a common identity. Otherwise different groups may act like fragmented tribes bickering and fighting with each other. For example, Americans, English and Australians have decided female circumcision is not allowed in their countries, even though it is a valued cultural practice of many of their citizens with African backgrounds. Similarly, Americans see gun ownership as a right. But in Britain or Australia citizens of American background have to conform to English and Australian restrictions on gun ownership.

Probably the most effective way in which a shared value system can be created in diverse communities is through a free, compulsory, non-secular education system. This provides a common influence on children that can reflect and teach common values of the new country while respecting cultural origins. In a State education system children have to learn to get along with differences. Intimate contact breaks down suspicion and isolation. However, this is only possible and effective when the whole community maintains a commitment to a high standard of State education that is trusted, promotes equality of opportunity, and is accountable to the community's common values.

Another way of promoting social cohesion is to make every individual feel that they matter and that what they think matters. One simple way of doing this is to make voting compulsory, which sends a strong message to every adult citizen that they have a responsibility to and are members of the community. It also encourages more representative government and therefore greater acceptance of government decisions and authority, which are essential for social cohesion. Because everybody votes, moderate opinions are represented — not just those of people with strong or extreme views, or powerful lobby groups. This system better reflects the community's values and leads to a balance in government decision-making.

There are many other issues and factors contributing to social cohesion. The rapidly increasing diversity of views and values proliferating in modern countries means that we urgently need to examine these factors. The radical changes now occurring in social and government policies throughout the world may have unexpected outcomes that could seriously erode social cohesion and connectedness, and that could compromise our capacity to be healthy and happy.

Explore your needs

It is quite common (and perfectly normal) to have times in your life when, in spite of family and friends, you feel lonely. Loneliness can be particularly acute when you are suddenly faced with a situation beyond the reach of those closest to you such as the loss of a job or a life-threatening illness. No matter how much those who love you may want to help or be able to empathise, it can be frightening to realise that ultimately you have to deal with the situation yourself. Others can support you, but they can't go through the operation or treatment or new job interviews for you.

In these situations, self-help groups – in which you get a chance to share your feelings and fears with others going through similar experiences – can be invaluable, and can make a real difference to your recovery and prognosis. Indeed, if you feel lonely and isolated by your expeience, don't hesitate to reach out to others who have shared experiences. It can literally save your life. However, use self-help groups only while they appear to be constructive. In the short term these groups can be invaluable, but in the long term they can undermine health and happiness.

An important part of recovery and rehabilitation is learning to be well again and regaining confidence. Unfortunately, the reality can be that the person recovering feels as though families and insurance companies are punishing their recovery with increased expectations and responsibilities, and decreased benefits. If you stay in a self-help group too long or the group's focus is illness – rather than wellness – orientated, then this can seriously undermine your emotional rehabilitation.

If you are scared of being well, seek professional help and carefully assess the subtle messages given by those who are supporting you.

If, however, you are perfectly well but lonely, work out whether it's a global loneliness in your whole life or just parts of your life.

The next step is to explore your attitude to relationships.

Getting connected

But on a more personal level, what do you do if you don't have a good social network? How do you make friends and form satisfying relationships?

Admit you want other people in your life. If you sit at home wishing and imagining you had friends or a close relationship, you'll never have one.

Explore your attitude to relationships

If you have been hurt in the past, been rejected or been too uncertain and shy to reach out to others, you need to have a good hard look at your self-talk and review the section on overcoming shyness (page 172). Become more realistic and focused on your positive qualities but also recognise that first visual impressions are extremely important.

> ℞ *Admit you want other people in your life. If you sit at home wishing and imagining you had friends or a close relationship, you'll never have one.* ℞

If you are careless with personal grooming and project an air of 'I don't care about myself', it will be impossible to attract people who want to respect you and who respect themselves. Instead you will attract other people who project an air of 'I don't care' or those who want to look after you, which in the long term can be disastrous.

Take time to develop self-talk that says:

- 'I'm worthwhile.'
- 'I'm entitled to enjoy satisfying friendships and relationships.'

- 'I like myself and I'm interested in other people.'
- 'I can enjoy other people.'

Once you have your beliefs about yourself and others sorted out, start working on your social skills.

Social skills

To connect with people, you need to be able to use the basic medium that connects people: conversation. Practise saying to yourself 'Hi, my name's ...' in an open, natural, friendly manner and with a *smile* on your face. As you speak to people, make the other person feel important by giving them your complete attention.

If you don't know anybody in a group, go on to say 'I haven't been to these meetings before but I'm really interested in golf, tortoises, world peace, saving trees ...' 'Are you new too?' 'Have you been before?'

This is a great starter because other new people immediately open up to someone who shares their own uncertainty; if they are old-timers, you can start asking open questions to get them talking and to help you mix.

Opening lines

If you ask a question make it open-ended, not closed. This means avoiding questions that have yes/no answers that can stop conversation dead, or answers that take the conversation nowhere. Instead of:

- 'How long have you been a member?'
- 'How long have you been interested in X?' ask questions such as:
- 'What can you tell me about this organisation?'
- 'How did you get interested in X?'

If you've struck somebody who is just not able to respond appropriately, don't take it personally: just move on and keep trying.

Practise these open questions on people and acquaintances you already have, for example the butcher, receptionist at work, colleagues and neighbours, until you feel quite confident that you can get other people talking. Apart from taking the pressure off you, focusing on others and what they say makes you less self-conscious and more relaxed in social situations generally.

Listen for self-disclosures that can take conversations into other areas, for example:

- 'I only took up golf when I changed jobs.'
  'Oh, what sort of work do you do?'

Finding people to be friends with

If you were looking for a job, you would approach the task in a logical, systematic way, matching your skills with what an employer is looking for.

In the same way, to connect with other people you have to appraise your interests, skills, needs and values and then match them up with places and organisations likely to attract this kind of person. But if you want to make friends, you have to first take the sign off your chest that says 'I'm lonely, I desperately need a friend/a mate/*someone*'. Similarly, saying to someone 'I couldn't live without you' implies that you are seeking a prop because your life is inadequate, rather than seeking someone to add spice to an already happy existence. If you think and say these things, your body language, roving gaze and desperate eye contact will scream at people almost as if you wore a sign or were shouting to all and sundry through a megaphone.

In studies on what attracts people to one another, the most important factor was that the other person appeared confident and comfortable with and within themselves, giving the impression that contact with others would be welcomed, rather than desperately sought because they couldn't bear being alone with themselves.

Your body language is the overwhelming factor in how people read your level of comfort with and within yourself. Fidgeting, nail-biting, folding your arms in front of you, putting your head back or down, and crossing your legs and stooping, all signal your discomfort.

Standing tall and still, with your hands in your pockets or by your sides, signifies that you feel safe and comfortable with yourself. Imagine someone you admire in real life or a movie character who always seems confident and calm. Really study their body language, their tone of voice and their facial expressions.

The best way to be relaxed about making friends is to focus on an activity rather than on merely meeting people. You can then go out to enjoy the activity and the meeting becomes secondary and a possible bonus. In this way you return home from each activity at least satisfied with the enjoyment of what you have done, regardless of whether you met a lot of potential friends. The doing of the moment makes you happy, not the potential outcome.

Nobody can meet all your needs

Don't put all your eggs in one basket. You can't find *one* group or *one* person to help fulfil all your social and emotional needs; the burden is too great for anyone. The more resources you have, the stronger you will be, because you will be more independent.

> ❧ *You can't find one group or one person to help fulfil all your social and emotional needs; the burden is too great for anyone.* ❧

That's not to say there may not be someone special in your life with whom you share a great deal, but really successful long-term relationships allow people to have individual interests and networks as well as those more closely shared.

In friendship there may be different individuals and groups that satisfy different aspects of your life: hobbies, sports, political and/or religious interests, spiritual needs. Allow yourself to develop two to three networks of support and mutual involvement, especially if you live alone. Relationships can be destroyed very quickly when you have unrealistic expectations and make demands of other people that are inappropriate or that they just can't meet. Accept people the way they are; don't try to turn them into who you want them to be. Focus on what you like about them, not on what you don't like or what you would like.

Appropriate disclosure

The most satisfying relationships become more intimate, and this can happen only if you are prepared to take appropriate risks and if you know you can survive quite well even if they don't turn out.

Baring your soul on the first night of a pottery

course will drive people away. But coffee afterwards may be appropriate for more personal conversation if the other person is initiating a move towards greater intimacy. With some people, however, coffee afterwards may mean a more intimate discussion on the intricacies of glazing!

Be sensitive to other people's needs and pace your relationship accordingly. If after a few weeks the conversation at squash is still strictly squash but you feel you'd like to know someone better, sound them out. 'I'm enjoying our squash games – would you like to join me for coffee afterwards?' If the response is negative because of other commitments, suggest a definite alternative time. If the person seems to hedge or is reluctant to make a firm commitment, take this to mean that they are not interested in a closer relationship. Accept their response, but don't then assume there is something wrong with you. They may really enjoy your company for squash but have family or other commitments that just don't allow closer ties, or they may simply have no need for more people in their life. That's OK! Let them see you are comfortable with this and enjoy what you do have with them; then seek a closer relationship elsewhere.

> Be sensitive to other people's needs and pace your relationship accordingly.

Developing intimacy

Developing intimate relationships requires some basic skills that you may need to learn or improve.

In order to be intimate with another person, you need to be able to observe, identify and express your own feelings. If you have been brought up in a family that does not express or share feelings, or that expects feelings to be actively suppressed, you may need to do some basic work on improving the language of feelings. Apart from 'happy', 'sad' and 'angry', how many words do you know that express feelings?

> In order to be intimate with another person, you need to be able to observe, identify and express your own feelings.

Try this exercise: sit comfortably and take a deep breath in ... and out ... and as you breathe out notice what you are feeling or what feeling you may like to have at that moment. If you can't identify it, read the list of feelings below to help you.

abandoned	amazed	awed
accepting	ambivalent	bad
adamant	angry	beautiful
adequate	annoyed	betrayed
affectionate	anxious	bitter
agonised	apathetic	blissful
almighty	astounded	bold

bored

brave

burdened

calm

capable

captivated

caring

challenged

charmed

cheated

cheerful

childish

clever

combative

competitive

condemned

confused

conspicuous

contented

contrite

cruel

crushed

culpable

deceitful

defeated

delighted

desirous

despairing

destructive

determined

different

diffident

diminished

discontented

distracted

disturbed

divided

dominated

dubious

eager

ecstatic

electrified

empty

enchanted

energetic

enervated

envious

evil

exasperated

excited

exhausted

fascinated

fearful

flustered

foolish

frantic

free

friendly

frightened

frustrated

full

furious

glad

good

gratified

greedy

grieving

groovy

guilty

gullible

happy

hateful

heavenly

helpful

helpless

high

homesick

honoured

horrible

hurt

hysterical

ignored

immortal

imposed upon

infuriated

inspired

intimidated

isolated

jealous

joyous

jumpy

keen

kind

kinky

laconic

lazy

lecherous

left out

licentious

lonely

longing

loving

low

lustful

mad

maudlin

mean

melancholy

miserable

mystical

naughty

nervous

nice

nutty

obnoxious

obsessed

odd

opposed

outraged

overwhelmed

pained

panicked

parsimonious

peaceful

persecuted

petrified

pitying

pleasant

pleased

precarious

pressured

pretty

prim

quarrelsome

queer

raging

rapturous

refreshed

rejected

relaxed

relieved

remorseful

restless

reverent

rewarded

righteous

sad

satiated

satisfied

scared

sceptical

screwed up

servile

settled

sexy

shocked

silly	sympathetic	trapped
sneaky	talkative	troubled
solemn	tempted	ugly
sorrowful	tenacious	vehement
spiteful	tender	violent
startled	tense	vital
stingy	tentative	vivacious
strange	tenuous	vulnerable
stuffed	terrible	weepy
stunned	terrified	wonderful
stupefied	threatened	wicked
stupid	thwarted	worried
sure	tired	zany

Now put these words that describe how you are feeling into sentences to express them. (It helps if you make a picture in your mind to express the feeling.) For example:

- 'I'm so unhappy my chest feels as if it's being crushed.'

- 'I'm so happy I feel light enough to fly.'

- 'I need tenderness, to feel loved, cared for, accepted.'

If you have a good friend or partner, practise expressing your feelings using the new words at your

> ☙ Relationships that are not given or allowed enough time or opportunity to develop through the four stages are rarely happy for both partners in the long term. ☙

disposal, and connecting them to bodily sensations and pictures in your mind.

Staying connected

Take your time over intimacy
A good intimate relationship can occur and endure only if you are prepared to be honest about yourself and respectful of the other person. It takes time to develop trust. Intimacy then develops in stages:

- acquaintanceship or getting to know someone superficially
- companionship where you may enjoy common interests
- friendship where trust develops and thoughts and feelings are shared
- loving sexual relationship.

Relationships that are not given or allowed enough time or opportunity to develop through these stages are rarely happy for both partners in the long term.

If you have been hurt in relationships, it is common to be scared of real intimacy ('If they know who I really am they won't like me any more'); so you avoid these stages and jump straight through to the going-to-bed stage. Such fear can lead to dishonesty, deceit and distrust. Manipulative ploys such as abuse, blame, shame and guilt, and passive aggression in forms such as not talking and emotional withdrawal, are often used to try to control the other person.

This kind of destructive relationship may never have been given the chance to grow at an appropriate pace for trust and hence real intimacy to develop, because both people were looking for instant gratification of desperate emotional and sexual needs.

People in a destructive relationship have unrealistic expectations. The relationship is dishonest and disrespectful and is very hard work.

Unrealistic expectations can also make trusting others difficult, as you can feel they are always letting you down. Because we all have a unique perspective on the world, someone is bound to disappoint you, whether intentionally or not. Protect yourself, but also try to give people the benefit of the doubt. Then trust yourself to be able to handle misunderstanding and even betrayal.

People in a healthy intimate relationship have realistic expectations and are not trying to solve problems or inadequacies in anyone's life. Such relationships tend to flow comfortably and easily.

It's very important to realise and remember that Western societies do not make it easy to establish longstanding relationships. Job mobility means that friendships and families constantly are being asked to suspend, re-establish and even break relationships. So any difficulties you are experiencing in creating a satisfying feeling of interconnectedness are not all your fault. More and more people are rejecting promotions and career pathways that disrupt these networks in their lives, preferring less-skilled jobs on less pay if necessary, to stay close to friends and family. These people know intrinsically what research has also discovered: a feeling of being closely interconnected with other human beings is more important for health and happiness than career or money.

Thank goodness for the common sense of ordinary people.

Make your neighbourhood more neighbourly

One of the most rewarding networks to be part of in your life is a good neighbourhood. Unfortunately, today's mobility means that on average people stay in one place only for four years. The days when generations were born, lived, worked and died in the one area are long gone. The need for two breadwinners in families also means that many neighbourhoods are deserted during the day. When people do come home, they are too tired and too busy meeting family commitments to be interested – let alone involved – in neighbourhood relationships.

But despite these difficulties, it's well worth considering whether a little effort could make your neighbourhood more neighbourly. Your aim is not to intrude on people's space but to create a friendly atmosphere that encourages co-operation and a feeling of belonging. Unfortunately, isolation from each other breeds wariness and suspicion, but if you reach out to be friendly

> ⟑ *Isolation from each other breeds wariness and suspicion, but if you reach out to be friendly you may be surprised at how much other people want to be friendly too.* ⟑

you may be surprised at how much other people want to be friendly too.

Here are some simple ways to create greater connectedness in your neighbourhood:

- Introduce yourself and your household to your neighbours on either side and opposite you.
- Offer to keep an eye on their property and check the letterbox if they go away.
- When someone new moves in, introduce yourself and give them some helpful local information, for example the best local general store, rubbish collection days, and so on.
- Hold a street/flats 'get-to-know-each-other' evening. Just drop friendly cards in letterboxes naming place and time and asking everyone to bring a plate of food to share. This can work especially well around public holidays, Christmas or New Year, when people's antisocial tendencies are weakened. In multicultural communities this can be a particularly 'delicious' way to meet neighbours.
- Have a friendly front fence and garden, not a six-foot solid barrier.
- Get a well-behaved dog and walk it. Friendly pets (and babies) are instant non-threatening topics of conversation.

- When you see someone in the street, smile and say 'hello' instead of looking poker-faced.
- Join a neighbourhood watch group.
- Lobby your local government to make people-focused policies a priority.

Even a highly mobile neighbourhood can become friendly and supportive with just a little effort. Many wonderful friendships develop and are even renewed among neighbours. One woman who took up my suggestion and held a street party discovered two old school friends living in the same street! The three of them had moved into the street within months of each other and had lived there for three years, not knowing of each other until the street party. What a reunion!

Avoid unnecessary conflict

Life would certainly be a lot more pleasant if we could avoid conflict. Unfortunately, as we all have our own unique perspectives and beliefs about ourselves and our worlds there are going to be inevitable differences of opinion, which are often based on these different perspectives.

Most people prefer, if they can, to avoid conflict. There are others, however, who not only seek it out, perhaps as an outlet for anger about other issues entirely, but who enjoy and even thrive on it! If you are forced to deal with these kinds of people, either personally or professionally, you need to be aware of a few strategies to minimise damage to yourself without letting them walk all over you or avoiding the issue.

Basically, to avoid conflict you need to try to understand other people's needs and fears and focus on solving the problem in a way that still tackles the issue but which, hopefully, also allays each party's fears and satisfies each party's needs.

> Once you start focusing on a collaborative approach to finding a solution rather than scoring points, it becomes more likely that you will come up with a win–win solution.

Once you start focusing on a collaborative approach to finding a solution rather than scoring points, it becomes more likely that you will come up with a win–win solution rather than an 'I win, you lose' or 'you win, I lose' situation. This, of course, assumes the other party isn't trying to use the situation to enhance their power by making you lose.

When negotiating with someone in a situation where there is a conflict of opinion, either ask the other person what it is they need to achieve (their needs) or work it out for yourself from what they are really saying to you. In the same way become aware of their fears. Angry people are usually frightened of something: loss of face, loss of power, loss of prestige, wasting time and energy ... At the same time, become aware of your own needs and fears in the situation. With reasonable people you can actually write these down and then brainstorm a collabora-

> ✒ *Angry people are usually frightened of something: loss of face, loss of power, loss of prestige, wasting time and energy ...* ✒

tive, satisfying solution or compromise. For example:

Me	*You*
• Needs:	• Needs:
• Fears:	• Fears:

To negotiate effectively you will need to:

- Give the conflict the time and energy needed to solve it.
- Sharpen up your skills of assertiveness so you are not sidetracked into irrelevant or personal issues.
- Decide that you would prefer a successful conclusion rather than the satisfaction of mutual failure.
- Neither attack nor judge the other party or their values personally.
- Be open to a full explanation of proposed solutions before judging them.
- Be aware that the other party may be under pressure from sources you are unaware of or do not understand.

ALEC AND HIS PARENTS – A CASE STUDY

Thirteen-year-old Alec and his parents were in conflict over his going out at night with friends. Instead of attacking each other's fears and concerns, they came up with a solution that satisfied all their needs, and allayed all their fears.

Before this could happen, though, the parents had to reveal to their son a lot more about their own fears for his safety and their legal responsibilities as parents. As a result, he could see they were not just being difficult and control-ling but that they cared deeply about his welfare and had other people they were accountable to as well. They also had to express their faith in him that he would not delib-erately seek out trouble but that, given the violent police record of one of the boys, he could find himself in an unex-pected situation that might put him and others in danger.

Incidentally, Alec was very reluctant to discuss the issue, particularly as it was more the norm to fight with parents than co-operate with them. But because his parents stayed calm and pointed out that if he wanted more freedom he had to display the maturity to discuss issues, he eventually cooled down enough (over some days of quiet, assertive persistence and use of the 'broken-record' technique (see page 140) by his parents) to draw up a table of respective needs and fears. (See table on page 291.)

The quiet calm of his parents in the face of his angry outbursts eventually got him to the point of discussing his own fears and needs. At this point some appropriate self-disclosure by his father and mother of the peer pressure they had felt as teenagers helped Alec realise his parents were after a solution: they were not attacking him for his need to be accepted or his fears of rejection.

The parents, at my suggestion, let Alec come up with most of the solutions so that he felt more empowered and

Son (Alec)	*Parents*
Needs:	Needs:
• To be more independent of parents.	• To know son is safe.
• To be accepted by peers.	• To be seen by community as responsible parents.
• To be seen by peers as independent.	
Fears:	Fears:
• Friends will see him as a wimp controlled by parents.	• Son will get into 'trouble' and put himself at risk; become uncontrollable; endanger others who try to help him if he's in danger.
	• They will be held entirely responsible by the community if he gets into trouble.

less controlled. In turn they concentrated a lot on statements like 'perhaps you might consider ...' and 'maybe you'd feel OK about ...'

Eventually Alec decided that if his friends thought that some of the decisions were coming from Alec himself they would be more acceptable than if they thought they were coming from his parents. Alec actually admitted that roaming the streets after dark was trouble waiting to happen. He decided to be more assertive about what he wanted to do as he often found the aimless roaming extremely boring anyway, and suspected some of the others did too.

Alec agreed to have his activities and destinations decided beforehand and to phone if there were any changes, not because he had to report in but because it was showing consideration for other people's feelings. He also agreed that if he saw trouble brewing he would immediately find an excuse to phone his parents and get a lift home.

Alec's parents were quite surprised at how resourceful he could be in coming up with ways that allowed him to save face but that also respected their concerns. But what surprised them most was that the more they presented him with their concerns or a problem, the more responsible his solutions became.

Alec did need help in becoming more assertive with his friends. He found that imagining himself as James Bond –

cool, calm, walking tall, not fussed by other people's tempers or personal insults – was successful when dealing with the stronger members of the group. Alec really enjoyed this role-playing (although I couldn't resist asking him to update James Bond's attitude to women) and he found it brilliantly successful with teachers.

James Bond was always comfortable about simply admitting embarrassing moments or being caught out, and this worked a treat with teachers:

'Yes, you're quite right. I should have done my homework.'

'You are quite correct. I did call the Assistant Principal a useless prick.'

We soon had to rein in Alec's new-found confidence a little!

The basis of resolving conflict is genuine mutual respect, and this requires not just commitment but time and energy. Consider the case of a volunteer working with well-paid administrators with no intention of resolving conflicts because they basically lack the necessary skills for the job. In this case their most basic fear is for their inadequacy to be discovered. In such situations, where the commitment of both parties is absent or there is a vast difference in the time and energy available to each party, conflict may be the only way of resolving the issue. But even in these circumstances, persistence can still solve the issue if you at least keep yourself focused and ignore attempts to personally attack and distract you.

> ℧ The basis of resolving conflict is genuine mutual respect, and this requires not just commitment but time and energy. ℧

However, you need to remain aware of what are the battles and what are the wars and to walk away if the power differential is such that a solution is impossible.

In short ...

℧ Be aware that, when it comes to health, your social and emotional environments are as important as the physical.

℧ If you are alone, it is helpful for you to become involved in social networks that will demand a contribution in terms of energy and commitment.

℧ Pets need to be cared for, and we need to be needed. Caring even for a goldfish can provide health benefits you never dreamed of. So get a companion creature, especially if you are alone.

🖋 Brush up on your conversation skills. Be open and friendly.

🖋 Look for friends where you are most likely to meet people with similar interests to your own.

🖋 Try to show that you are fairly independent. The stronger you seem, the more attractive you will be to others.

🖋 Don't wear your heart on your sleeve. A needy person can come across as a potential burden.

🖋 Let the friendship move at its own pace. Give it a chance to develop some depth.

🖋 If conflict arises, try to use and encourage a co-operative approach. Aim for a win–win solution.

🖋 Think about how you could promote a neighbourly feeling in your neighbourhood and your community.

The 8th Secret: Healthy people are flexible people

Flexibility can be strength

Imagine you are eating a jelly baby. Initially it feels rather soft and squishy, but notice how long it takes to chew the jelly baby until nothing is left. Although it is soft and yielding, it's also extremely tough. The flexibility of the jelly baby is what makes it resistant to the pressure of your teeth.

> ❧ *People who are ruled by* rigid shoulds *and* should nots *are resistant to* maybes. ❧

Now imagine you are eating a potato chip. One crunch and it disintegrates. Its very hardness makes it extremely brittle.

Your ability to cope emotionally and physically with life and to be healthy and happy is very much determined by how flexible or how rigid you are in your behaviour, perceptions and beliefs. To become more flexible in your approach to life, go back and look at the common distorted thinking patterns and how to change them (see page 49). For instance, people who are ruled by rigid *shoulds* and *should nots* are resistant to *maybes*. This black-and-white thinking, which we have discussed before, defies reality: the world is made up of constantly changing shades of grey. In the real world, whether we like it or not, the goalposts *do* keep shifting. Remind yourself that although change is inherently stressful because it requires you to adjust and adapt, it is not necessarily distressful. Having to change can be a eu-stress experience; that is, a powerful, positive stress in your life. It is not uncommon for heart attack patients to say that their attack was the most terrifying, but also the most positive experience of their lives because they were forced to change their priorities. Changing priorities can lead to a more fulfilling and emotionally rewarding lifestyle.

> *In the real world, whether we like it or not, the goalposts do keep shifting.*

If you can develop an attitude that accepts the changes that occur, your energy will be better directed to dealing with them, whether they be modifying your perceptions, your beliefs or your subsequent behaviour. The flexible person lives longer and more happily.

JILLIAN – A CASE STUDY

Jillian was 48 years old with three teenage daughters. Her husband had died after a very long illness. She and her daughters missed him terribly but were all delighted when Jillian met a man named Gary and fell deeply in love. Unfortunately, Gary had a rather worrying past: he had physically and emotionally abused his first wife and children, and had been a violent alcoholic. He had attended AA and had been successfully 'dry' for many years. Although he had a steady job, he had no assets to contribute to the relationship. Jillian had been brought up in a strict fundamentalist

Christian family and was still actively committed to her religion. However, she was extremely worried that even though Gary appeared to be the perfect partner *now*, things might change if they married. If the marriage didn't work or if Gary started drinking again, she would be putting herself and her daughters in a precarious position – physically, emotionally, and financially.

Under the circumstances, it would seem that living together for a while was a possible solution; it would help her determine whether or not Gary was able to handle a closer relationship. But on the other hand, Jillian's religion would not allow such an arrangement. She was torn: obey the strict and rigid code of her religion or be more flexible in response to the difficult circumstances.

After much soul-searching, she and Gary started living together. She was banished from her church, which she had expected and accepted, but for six months the family was happy. Then Gary's working hours were reduced and he was forced to work only part time. He started drinking again and began abusing Jillian and her girls.

Even though she still loved Gary, Jillian was not prepared to have herself or her girls abused under any circumstances, so she had Gary forcibly removed from the house. Their separation was a relatively simple matter because they weren't married. Although distraught that the relationship had ended and that it had also cost her the love and support of her church, Jillian felt that by being flexible she had saved herself and her children from possibly years of trauma trying to dissolve a marriage. She could only have become more flexible in her thinking by being prepared to look at the appropriateness of old rules to new situations.

There are many personal rules that may be entirely appropriate at one stage of our lives but which are totally inappropriate at another. To become more flexible, give yourself permission to assess the changes in your life or circumstances and make modifications to your rule book. When modifying or changing rules, have the integrity to make rules based on appropriate respect for yourself and for others. This may not necessarily be in accordance with what those close to you want or expect, but claim the right to find a balance with what is relevant *now*, rather than with what is relevant to another culture or another age.

In short ...

🖋 Beware the black-and-white approach to life — nothing is ever that simple.

🖋 Practise being flexible: you'll last much longer.

The 9th Secret: Healthy people feel they have an important role in life

The right to feel useful

You may know of someone who retired in apparent good health and then died within a few months. Those whose work has provided not just an income but a way of life, and almost their entire social circle, are particularly at risk.

HAROLD – A CASE STUDY

Harold was an outback policeman. For thirty years he was the only policeman within a radius of fifty miles in a remote area of Australia with an eclectic mix of nationalities and cultures. He was a big man with a quiet, relaxed manner. His size and calm demeanour had quietened and resolved many violent and explosive situations. His tolerant and flexible attitude to the law was admired, respected and much-needed in such an isolated community. He constantly received warm appreciation of his skill as a peacemaker as well as a law-keeper.

Harold's whole life was his job. He was on call twenty-four hours a day and had sometimes gone for two years without a holiday if relief staff couldn't be found. Everything he did was related to his work. And despite being a smoker for all of his adult life, an enthusiastic imbiber of the amber fluid, and a steak-chips-and-fried-eggs addict, he was extraordinarily fit and healthy.

Then Harold retired. Within six months his hair had gone completely white; he developed rheumatoid arthritis, and then heart failure. In nine months he was dead. At his well-attended funeral everyone commented on how shocked they had been to see his rapid deterioration. But, as his wife said, he really died when he retired and lost all purpose for living.

While financial plans for retirement should be made throughout your adult working life, emotional plans for retirement need to start ten to fifteen years before you actually retire. This is especially important if your job is also your hobby and your social life.

Make time to start exploring other interests and develop a social network separate from work. For some people, other interests actually become small businesses or positions of responsibility in community organisations. For others, further education becomes a deeply rewarding occupation that keeps them highly stimulated.

Alternatively, don't retire. Do you *want* to retire? Perhaps you would prefer to work part time and still have the commitment but greater flexibility, or gradually cut down your hours over some years before you fully retire. This gives you the chance to explore other interests but keeps you connected to old networks while you do it.

Retrenchment can also be deadly or at the very least increase the risk of serious physical illness or depression. We all need to feel that we are useful, that our life counts, that our contribution would be missed. It does not appear to be enough for most people to be simply busy, to be seen as useful; activity has to have some kind of social and public recognition in its usefulness, which commonly means being paid for what you do.

> ❧ We all need to feel that we are useful, that our life counts, that our contribution would be missed. ❧

A study of women who filled their lives with activities such as lunching with friends, aerobic classes, charity work and pottery classes found that they were not nearly as healthy or happy as another sample of women who had at least a part-time job paying a proper salary.

A group of teenage mothers were found to have better all-over health and happiness, despite the poverty and difficulty of single parenting, than unemployed girls of the same age. The perceived usefulness of being mothers with an important role overrode the practical difficulties.

The recent appearance of 'structural unemployment' in Western societies, especially among the young, shows a disturbing callousness on the part of the rest of society towards those unable to fulfil what has become a very basic human social need. An overwhelming body of research has shown that where there is high unemployment there are higher rates of suicide, cardiovascular disease and marital breakdown, and this is worse for those in communities with poor social cohesion. There is often an attitude of indifference shown by those who have a job and those with a network of contacts to secure jobs for their children, towards those in a less powerful position.

It's disturbing to hear economists say that an unemployment level of 5–6 per cent is good because it prevents a push for higher wages. Good for whom? Those who are in work and have access to the good things in life, and who declare that people really could work if they wanted to, deny the reality that economists and governments feel comfortable with a certain level of unemployment – as long as it's not too high to affect voting preferences.

> ❧ *Where there is high unemployment there are higher rates of suicide, cardiovascular disease and marital breakdown, and this is worse for those in communities with poor social cohesion.* ❧

High unemployment existing while many employed people are oveworked, is not a new phenomenon. The industrial revolution created similar problems, which were resolved by reducing working hours. The current technological revolution means that we can now reduce working hours again, and share the work and the benefits. Apart from creating employment, which is so important to health and happiness, it would allow everyone to achieve a healthier and happier balance in their lives. A better balance also improves productivity. Other spin-offs are more jobs in the leisure industry, more taxes for governments and a smaller social security bill.

As a further bonus, reduced working hours would enable women to participate more fully in jobs with influence and power. They would no longer be competing with men who work ridiculous hours because they have a supportive wife at home. Children would have better access to their dads as well as to their mums, and the community would have better access to a better balance of views, skills and practices in positions of power.

Yet, for rather vague reasons some economists are surprisingly resistant to the idea of reducing working hours. Perhaps they have a problem with change?

Because we do live in communities, we are all ultimately affected by the consequences of some people having no role and no job: the social unrest, crime, and addictive behaviours that increase in unemployed groups affect the safety and insurance premiums of us all. The effects of the unhappiness, misery and ill health of these groups ripple through our social pond, draining our collective resources.

There will always be people who will take advantage of 'safety net' social programs designed to look after those less fortunate, but that kind of abuse can be controlled and is in reality quite minor. A community that risks some abuse of this system but that cares for others when they are sick and gives them a helping hand *to help themselves* when fate, economics or lack of personal competency and skills robs them of the basic need to be needed and to be of value to the community, provides its citizens with a better opportunity to be healthy and happy than a community that turns its back on people in need.

In short ...

- Be aware that you have the right to feel useful, and to be rewarded for your contribution to the community.

- Learn how to gain access to resources and to use them for your benefit.

- Let policy-makers know that the needs of ordinary people are important.

The 10th Secret: Healthy people feel part of something bigger than themselves

Shared values and beliefs

Being part of a social group and social network is undoubtedly beneficial to your health. Cultures and religions that encourage independence and commitment to shared values and beliefs have healthier, happier members than individuals with no such commitment. The very structure of these groups makes it easier for people to feel that their place in the group is relevant and important to the benefit of all.

> ❧ Being part of a social group and social network is undoubtedly beneficial to your health. ❧

But the benefit of such groups can be dramatically undermined if individuals do not have a sense of personal control or if they feel they are being used. This often becomes apparent in dictatorships, extreme fundamentalist groups, cults or other organisations that masquerade as being for mutual benefit but are in fact for the benefit of only a few. People are initially attracted to these groups because of the very powerful need in all of us to think that our life is important and has meaning, and more importantly, that we are part of something bigger than ourselves.

Be wary of groups that promote their members as being 'specially chosen by God' for some extremely important role, for example working for world peace, saving the environment, or spreading the word about a particular belief system. Anyone who is not satisfied with their social and community network or who feels life lacks real satisfaction and meaning can be very vulnerable to such groups and find themselves involved in some rather unusual or potentially devastatingly damaging groups.

If you don't feel happy with the relationships in your life or your days' lack of purpose in the short and long term, recognise this need in yourself and think carefully about how it could be filled. There is no need to become involved in groups that promise happiness 'if you believe X' and 'when you do Y'. There are so many other organisations and groups

> There are many organisations and groups that allow you to be happy each moment now – without the conditions of 'if' or 'when'.

that play a genuinely important role, that give you a sense of belonging, and that allow you to be happy each moment *now* — without the conditions of 'if' or 'when'.

A measurable boost in the immune system was found in people watching a video of Mother Teresa doing her charity work in India. How much healthier and happier would you be if you chose to allow yourself to become part of something much bigger than yourself?

Part of the debriefing process for emergency service

workers following a bushfire, earthquake or other
natural disaster involves helping people come to terms
with the let-down feeling of no longer being involved
with others to achieve a common and shared goal. Many
volunteer workers find this let-down feeling takes weeks
or even months to get over. Despite the horror and
tragedy of what they have been through, they can still
miss that sense of bonding that comes from being mobilised to meet a desperate community need.

There is a deep personal satisfaction and enrichment
that comes from thinking not just of yourself. However, when doing voluntary work, be careful that you
are not being taken advantage of by either the group
or the community. With the move to a smaller and
smaller government, volunteers are increasingly being
asked to do work that the community previously paid
for, such as school maintenance, park maintenance,
and fostering children. Abusing people's willingness
and need to help others will ultimately not make an
individual or a community healthier or happier. If we
take advantage of people's generosity, over time we
create a seething resentment and people turn away
from all voluntary work for fear of being used.

But if you find yourself feeling that despite a
happy family, job, friends, reasonable health and
material possessions there is still 'something missing',

it may be a good idea to look around the community and see if you can become involved in an activity where your efforts will be respected and appreciated: conservation, politics, charities, voluntary work, land care, tree-planting, environmental clean-up days. When you become involved, focus on enjoying each moment of *doing* rather than on the final outcome. Imagine what a world it would be if we could mobilise all the energy from our need to belong and be involved in something bigger than just ourselves!

The need to believe

The way many people become involved in something more significant than themselves is through religion. The concept of a usually benevolent higher authority or 'god' who knows what's going on and the reasons for it (even if those reasons are unknown to mortals), is extremely comforting for many people. Religion can also bring structure and rhythm to people's lives with daily rituals, and special days and times of the year. It can provide instant bonding, commitment and responsibility to others of the same faith

> ℞ *Religion can bring structure and rhythm to people's lives with daily rituals, and special days and times of the year.* ℞

and value system, which can bring certainty and security to one's life. For many, religion also provides a ready-made purpose or special role in life and this can compensate for the tedium of a burdensome job or other unsatisfying aspects of their lives.

Even allowing for restrictive lifestyle factors – a strict diet, or no alcohol or extramarital sex – being an active participant in a benevolent religious faith can be good for the body as well as for the soul.

If organised religion is not your thing, however, or if as a woman you find it too patriarchal, all these good things about religion can still be had through involvement with community and international groups, and by establishing your own set of beliefs about yourself and the world. A modern Muslim woman friend feels no need to cover her head or to strictly obey dietary laws, but she still observes many of her religious rituals, fasting and reading of her Koran. She finds it impossible to comprehend how I could 'live', let alone be happy, with no religious rules or faith in my life.

> If organised religion is not your thing, all the good things about religion can still be had by establishing your own set of beliefs about yourself and the world.

Yet I do have rules, rituals and faith. I have a very strong feeling of interconnectedness with my environment and all things in it. My four p.m. cup of tea in a particular china cup is a ritual and a family joke. I like routine and structure in my life, but I also like enough spontaneity and novelty to make it stimulating. I have my own rules and set of ethics, which I strictly adhere to. But I recognise the fact that, like many other people, I have the sort of personality that needs to find its own rules. I'm not very good at following other people's and would feel confined and manipulated if I did.

So try to find the 'god' that suits you, as well as a social network that needs you and that you can be committed to. Being part of something 'bigger' is empowering and makes you healthier and happier.

In short …

ᘰ Being part of something bigger than yourself can be an empowering experience. It can enhance your health.

ᘰ Don't fall for promises that you'll be happy 'if you believe …' or 'when you do …' You can reasonably expect to be happy *now* without these conditions. Live in the moment.

🖋 Look about you. What can you do to help your community and so have a sense of belonging?

🖋 If organised religion doesn't appeal to you, there's nothing to stop you from developing your own code of beliefs, or from setting up rituals to give shape to your days.

PART FOUR

Secrets of Peace of Mind
and Contentment

The 11th Secret:
The secret of peace of mind

Matching perceptions to beliefs

Perhaps the chief underlying reason that people seek the help of professionals like myself, that drives sales of personal development books skyward and is causing a boom in personal growth courses worth billions of dollars a year throughout the Western world, is a search for that elusive state called peace of mind.

ROSLYN – A CASE STUDY

Roslyn had grown up the eldest of four girls in a loving family with little money. Although bright, she was not as talented or as physically attractive as her sisters. Being the eldest, she was far more aware of her parents' financial struggle as they worked long hours in a family business. At thirteen she was given and readily accepted a great deal of responsibility for her younger sisters.

Roslyn spent her teenage years feeling that for her life was hard work and for her sisters life was carefree. While they revelled in teenage trivia, she saw herself as the responsible one who had to think of the consequences rather than of spontaneous and immediate pleasure. Her parents noticed how serious she was for her age and tried hard to get her to go out and enjoy herself. However, being responsible and serious became an escape for Roslyn. If she didn't show interest in dressing up, hairstyles, and boyfriends, she didn't have to compete or compare herself with her bubbly sisters.

When she left home, Roslyn's lack of self-acceptance led her on a giddying roundabout of self-improvement courses, and when that didn't make her feel better she became involved in a number of causes where she could continue to be a martyr and escape herself.

Despite having many friends, being involved in rather worthwhile causes, enjoying a well-paid and satisfying job, and possessing the ability to meditate and make her mind still 'whenever she felt like it', Roslyn was still very restless, often irritable and a long way from contentment and peace of mind.

Over time her restless pursuit of inner peace increasingly spilled over into her conversation. She became more and more preoccupied with 'sorting herself out'. The constant self-analysis and preoccupation with the dynamics of relationships began to bore her friends and turned new acquaintances away. The more preoccupied she became with herself, the more isolated she became from her family and her old friends. Soon the only people she could relate to were other restless and tortured souls unable to accept themselves and obsessed with what they didn't have.

I met Roslyn when she asked me to speak to a self-awareness and personal growth group she belonged to. In the group were fifteen men and women just as disgruntled as she was. Their emotional suffering was well masked by a veneer of love for each other: there was much hugging and touching, and faces that constantly smiled with over-bright, searching eyes that appeared to be saying 'I dare you to challenge how happy I think I am'.

Here was a group of extremely vulnerable people trying to convince themselves that they were OK and that the rest of the world had problems. I could have chosen to speak safe platitudes, confirming their misconceptions about themselves and others. Alternatively, I could gently get them to confront some of their beliefs and perceptions, enabling at least some of them to begin thinking in a way that might bring about genuine peace of mind and contentment, without the continual isolation from their old friends and family.

I chose the latter course. My talk had been scheduled for one hour with fifteen minutes of questions. Four hours later their initial anger and hostility turned to delight as they realised what real peace of mind and contentment were, and just how easily they could achieve them.

In some cultures peace is sought predominantly through prayer in various organised religions. However, a study found that 71 per cent of Australians sought and felt peace sitting by the sea, whereas only 29 per cent found peace in prayer or religion. In a wonderful understatement the head of this study, Dr Philip Hughes, a Uniting Church Minister, commented that the culture of prayer and church services was not very 'endearing' to many Australians.

For many other people, peace of mind becomes an escape into other altered states of awareness such as meditation (make your mind still) and self-hypnosis. There are, however, many people who have spent a small fortune on various meditation classes but who still can't meditate and still feel anguished. There are also people who, according to EEGs, can meditate extremely well but when not meditating still feel miserable.

> For many people, peace of mind becomes an escape into other altered states of awareness.

This may support quite fascinating research that has shown 'not thinking' and 'keeping your mind still' is not the way to find peace or happiness. When people make their 'mind still', they turn down activity in their left brain and enhance activity in the right brain. However, studies using positron emission tomography (PET) have found the exact opposite: people feel peaceful and happier when the left brain is active.

PET scanning of the brain creates computer-generated colour pictures of the brain while the brain is working. Glucose attached to radioactive isotopes is injected into the bloodstream and as the brain uses up the glucose the isotopes released give off radioactivity, which is read by the PET scanner. Where the greatest colour density occurs is where the brain is most active.

People looking at warm, loving pictures and beautiful scenery felt peaceful and happier and it was their left brain that was working. Looking at fearful, miserable pictures engendered feelings of unhappiness and restlessness, and activated the right brain.

Feeling peaceful and happier appears to require active thinking, which is exactly what we have discussed earlier: controlling your thoughts controls your feelings.

When your perceptions match up with your beliefs, you will feel real peace of mind.

So what is peace of mind and how do you achieve it?

When your perceptions about people and the world around you match up with your beliefs about people and the world, you will feel real peace of mind. That is, what you see matches what you believe.

For instance, if you, like Roslyn and her friends, believe that life should be fair, then every time you turn on the television, read a newspaper, talk to a neighbour or pass an accident on the road, you will be confronted with a perception (your reality) that shows life isn't fair. Your perception of life as being brutally unfair will not match your belief that it should be. This conflict between what you see and what you believe is what creates the turmoil and anguish within us. Or if you believe that bad things shouldn't happen to nice people, again you will be constantly confronted with the perception (your reality) that awful things can happen to the nicest people. Similarly, if you believe you are a good person, and therefore people should treat you well, experiences (perception) that being good to others doesn't automatically guarantee good deeds in return will be deeply disturbing.

> ❧ Match what you believe with what you actually see and experience around you. You can do this by either modifying your beliefs or modifying your perceptions. Modifying beliefs and perceptions doesn't mean giving up ideals and values. ❧

The secret to attaining peace of mind is to match your beliefs with your perceptions: match what you believe with what you actually see and experience around you.

You can do this by either modifying your beliefs or modifying your perceptions. This does not necessarily mean deluding yourself and going around with rose-coloured glasses perched permanently on the end of your nose (although a little bit of denial seems to be a rather good coping strategy). Modifying beliefs and perceptions doesn't mean giving up ideals and values. What it does mean is looking carefully at your self-talk and your perceptions and perhaps modifying them.

For instance, in regard to fairness, you will feel a great deal more peaceful within yourself if you can say:

- Life is not fair (more accurate perception), but it would be good if we all worked towards making it fairer (belief). Here your belief matches better with what you actually see happening (perception).

OR

- Being nice to people is contagious (belief) and can increase the possibility of people being nice to you in return (perception). Again the belief more accurately reflects the reality.

If you believe there should be no such thing as terminal illness in children, you will be far more anguished by the plight of a terminally ill child than will someone who can accept that this can and does happen.

When my brother was in his late teens, he developed a suspected malignant melanoma in his eye that could have been fatal within a very short period of time. A definitive diagnosis could be made only during surgery. When my grandmother was told that her only grandson, whom she loved dearly, could have a potentially fatal illness, her reaction astounded us. We were all worried sick, but she quite calmly said, 'What bad luck. Life can be so unfair and we'll all just have to deal with whatever happens. But let's hope for the best'. She then launched into talking about her strawberry crop.

Her reaction had the most extraordinarily calming effect on me; I was no longer fighting the belief that this should not happen to someone as wonderful as my brother. When we found out he did not have a life-threatening problem my grandmother said, 'I'm glad we didn't waste a lot of energy worrying too much'.

Considering my grandmother's extremely traumatic childhood and adult life, and her appalling diet where she subsisted on tea with eight teaspoons of sugar several times a day for as long as I can remember, it's extraordinary that she lived to eighty-four, surviving some awful illnesses in her eighties that should have killed her many times over.

But despite many bouts of severe depression as an

adult, which were due to the circumstances of her life, she always bounced back with the most delicious and wicked sense of humour! I think she had suffered so much emotional pain that by the time she was an adult she accepted and expected it, and so she no longer fought circumstances. In this way she suffered much less anguish than the rest of us.

If you feel in turmoil about a particular issue or you are just generally upset, try the following to achieve peace of mind:

- Write down the 'I/he/she should' and the 'I/he/she should not' statements underlying your beliefs about what is happening.

- Then write down what you actually see around you.

- Now modify the beliefs that are intrinsic in your 'should' and 'should not' statements to still retain your values and ideals. Introduce words and phrases such as 'perhaps', 'maybe', 'could be', 'would like it to be', 'influences', 'aim for'. Avoid dogmatic, inflexible language. Sometimes your actual values and priorities need to be examined and updated. Are you accepting what you can't change or hell-bent on fighting it?

- Look at your perceptions. Are they distorted in any way? Do you have past experiences that are influencing how you judge this situation (for example you left an abusive relationship and now in any encounter with the opposite sex you are looking for the hurt)? Are you blowing things up out of proportion? Ask yourself how much this will really matter in five years, ten years, fifty years, one hundred years from now. Are you using any of the distorted thinking patterns I discussed earlier in looking at self-talk (see page 49)? If necessary, juggle your perceptions to match your beliefs.

Peace of mind can be yours *right now*, no matter who you are or what you are doing. You can feel wonderfully peaceful when you are doing things and living life, not when you are running away from it.

> ❧ *Peace of mind can be yours* right now, *no matter who you are or what you are doing.* ❧

In short ...

❧ A brain in neutral doesn't equal peace of mind. You'll be happier with active thoughts, so long as these thoughts are under *your* control. Remember, control your thoughts and you control your feelings.

❧ Be more flexible. Be prepared to modify your beliefs and perceptions in relation to what you see in the world around you. Crying 'It isn't fair' won't get you peace of mind.

❧ Don't think you have to give up your ideals and values. Look at your self-talk and explore ways of modifying your beliefs and perceptions so that they match.

❧ If you think things are not fair in the world around you, see what you can *do* about it. This will empower you and make you feel less helpless.

The 12th Secret:
The secret of contentment

Adjusting your focus

Daniel Myers, a foremost 'happiologist', commented that 'happiness is less a matter of getting what you want than wanting what you have', but I think that statement says even more about contentment.

Being contented means feeling satisfied with your life. This is possible only if you can distinguish between needs and wants. The whole of this book is based on the premise that a person's basic needs for food, shelter and emotional and physical safety are being met. What we think are other needs are often really desires or wants based on comparing ourselves and what we have with others and what they have.

> 'Happiness is less a matter of getting what you want than wanting what you have.'

This was the basis of Roslyn's and many of her

group's discontent. They constantly looked at the hole rather than at the doughnut, to see what they didn't have compared with other people. Hence they were unable to see some quite special things in themselves and in their own lives.

In Roslyn's case, looking at the doughnut rather than at the hole suddenly revealed to her how distorted many of her beliefs and perceptions about herself and other people had been, especially about her sisters. To my surprise, she started mentioning quite tragic and awful events in her sisters' lives that she had previously never really acknowledged to herself. None of her sisters had had lives that were beds of roses; in fact, they had all been extremely prickly! Suddenly Roslyn was able to realise that they had worked hard to overcome many difficulties: severe dyslexia, sexual assault, the death of a fiancé.

> ✎ To be contented is to focus very much on the moment and on what you have. ✎

To be contented is to focus very much on the moment and not to say 'I'll feel satisfied when . . .', or 'I'll be satisfied if . . .'

To feel contented: *focus on this moment and on what you have*, not on what you don't have.

Try it right now. Are you prepared to choose to allow yourself to feel contented right now? Do you feel you deserve or have the right to feel contented right now?

Experiment with statements such as 'It might be nice to have X but I can choose to allow myself to be comfortable, contented and happy with what I have right now'. Imagine a big screen filled with all aspects of your life at this moment and imagine adjusting what you have so that it expands on the screen to fill in any gaps that you put there before. You could adjust the focus so that what you have shrinks, leaving gaping blank spaces, and all you see is everything that is missing. Or you can adjust the focus so that what you have expands and overlaps to fill the entire screen, causing you to feel overwhelming satisfaction and contentment with such a full life.

Peace of mind and contentment are possible right now. Simply choose to allow yourself to feel them.

In short ...

📎 Learn to distinguish between needs and wants or desires.

📎 Focus on the moment and on what you have.

📎 Be prepared to *allow* yourself to be contented.

📎 Remember, you deserve to feel contented, not 'when ...' or 'if ...', but right now. The choice is *yours*.

Conclusion: Knowledge is power

Knowing what makes people healthy and happy gives us the power to recognise, demand and strive for the kind of community that promotes health and happiness. We can firmly and confidently push the economists and accountants off centre stage and into the wings where they belong: as stage hands, not as principal players. We no longer need to be intimidated and mesmerised by the bean counters and their jargon; their gobbledygook doesn't have to distract us anymore. The bottom line is how does a policy impact on what we know is needed to enable people to live healthier and happier lives?

We need politicians, policies and actions that show respect, empathy, care and a willingness to share what the community produces. In an atmosphere of genuine mutual respect and mutual responsibility, all sections of the community can feel accepted and included.

In multicultural communities the personal qualities

and integrity of leaders become particularly important in order to set the standard for a climate of appropriately tolerant behaviour, and behaviour that allows and deliberately promotes social connectedness and social cohesion, which are so crucially important to health and happiness. So take your right to vote seriously: take control and influence the priorities and style of leaders and government.

But the most important keys to health and happiness are these: have an appropriate awareness of the future and the consequences of your actions, but choose to allow yourself to focus on the moment so that the moments become seconds, become minutes, become hours, become days, become years, become a happier, healthier life. Understand the continuous chain reaction of perceptions, beliefs, self-talk, feelings and behaviour that you can control. As long as your basic needs for food, shelter and safety are met, you can permit yourself to feel happier and more content regardless of your circumstances. You can use bad feelings to recognise, acknowledge, and accept needs and fears that you can overcome alone or by reaching out to others.

Being happier and healthier means not living in a cloud of denial but passionately and fully embracing a rich mixture of experiences and feelings; it means knowing you have within you, or can reach out to, whatever you need to help you deal with life. But above all else, it means deciding to allow yourself to be happier and healthier RIGHT NOW!

Further reading

Burns, David D., *Feeling Good*, Signet, New York, 1981.

Gray, John, *Men Are from Mars, Women Are from Venus*, Thorsons, London, 1993.

Ornstein, Robert & Sobel, David, *The Healing Brain*, Simon and Schuster, New York, 1987.

Samways, Louise, *The Chemical Connection*, Greenhouse Publications, Melbourne, 1989 (available from author).

Samways, Louise, *Your Mindbody Energy*, Viking, Melbourne, 1992.

Samways, Louise, *Dangerous Persuaders*, Penguin, Melbourne, 1994.

Seligman, Martin E. P., *Learned Optimism*, Random House, 1992.

Seligman, Martin E. P., *The Optimistic Child*, Random House, Sydney, 1995.

Smith, Manuel J., *When I Say No I Feel Guilty*, Bantam, New York, 1975.

Tannen, Deborah, *You Just Don't Understand*, William Morrow, New York, 1990.

For tapes on general relaxation, ideodynamic healing and sleeping better, write to Louise Samways, 1537 Nepean Highway, Rosebud West, Victoria, 3940, Australia.

Bibliography

Argyle, M., 'Anatomy of relationship rules', *British Journal of Psychology*, Nov. 1985.

Argyle, M., 'Happiness', *British Journal of Psychology*, Nov. 1991.

Bartrop, R., Lazarus, L., Luckhurst, E., et al., 'Depressed lymphocyte function after bereavement', *Lancet*, Vol. I, 1977.

Beardsley, G. & Goldstein, M. G., 'Psychological factors affecting physical condition: Endocrine disease literature review', *Psychosomatics* 34, 1993.

Beecher, Sabine, *Happiness: It's up to you*, Collins Dove, Melbourne, 1988.

Bentall, R., 'A proposal to classify happiness as a psychiatric condition', *Journal of Medical Ethics*, June 1992.

Borysenko, Joan, *Minding the body, mending the mind*, Bantam, New York, 1988.

Brinkman, Rick & Kirschner, Rick, *Dealing with people you can't stand*, McGraw-Hill, New York, 1994.

Cade, C. Maxwell & Coxhead, Nona, *The awakened mind*, Delacorte Press, New York, 1979.

Calabrese, J. R., Kling, M.A. & Gold, P. W., 'Alterations in immunocompetence during stress, bereavement and depression:

Focus on neuroendocrine regulation', *American Journal of Psychiatry* 144, 1987.

Carney, R. M., Rich, M. W. & Freedlake, K. E., 'Major depressive disorder predicts cardiac events in patients with coronary artery disease', *Psychosomatic Medicine* 50: 627–33, 1988.

Cassel, J., 'The contribution of the social environment to host resistance', *American Journal of Epidemiology* 104, 1976.

Davis, Martha, Eshelman, Elizabeth & McKay, Mathew, *The relaxation and stress reduction workbook*, 3rd ed., New Harbinger Publications, Oakland, 1988.

Diener, E., 'The road to happiness', *Psychology Today*, July/Aug. 1994.

Diener, E., 'Subjective wellbeing', *Psychological Bulletin*, May 1984.

Diener, E., 'Who is happy?', *Psychological Science* 1995.

Diener, E. & Myers, D., 'The secrets of happiness', *Psychology Today*, July/Aug. 1992.

Diener, E. & Myers, D., 'Who is Happy?', *Psychological Science*, Jan. 1995.

Douillard, John, *Body, mind and sport*, Harmony Books, New York, 1994.

Dreikers, Rudolf, *Happy children*, Collins/Fontana, London, 1972.

Eisenberg, D. M., Delbanco, T. L., Berkey, C. S., et al., 'Cognitive behavioural techniques for hypertension', *Annals Internal Medicine* 118, 1993.

Ell, K., Michimoto, R., Mediansky, L., et al., 'Social relations, social support and survival among patients with cancer', *Journal of Psychosomatic Research* 36, 1992.

Epstein, M., 'Opening up to happiness', *Psychology Today*, July/Aug. 1995.

Erikson, Milton H., *An uncommon casebook*, W. W. Norton & Company, New York, 1990.

Fawzy, F. I., Fawzy, N. W., Hyun, C. S., et al., 'Malignant melanoma: Effects of an early structured psychiatric intervention, coping and effective state on recurrence and survival six years later', *Archives General Psychiatry* 50: 1993.

Genova, Jackie, *Work that body*, Corgi Transworld, London, 1983.

Goldner, F., 'Pronoia', *Social Problems*, Oct. 1982.

Hartley-Brewer, Elizabeth, *Positive parenting*, Cedar/Mandarin, London, 1994.

Hawton, Keith, Salkovskis, Paul, Kirk, Joan & Clark, David, eds, *Cognitive behaviour therapy for psychiatric problems*, Oxford University Press, Oxford, 1990.

Irwin, M., Daniels, M., Bloom, E. T., et al., 'Life events, depressive symptoms and immune function', *American Journal of Psychiatry* 144, 1987.

Kanarch, T., Jennings, J. R., 'Biobehavioural factors in sudden cardiac death', *Psychological Bulletin* 109, 1991.

Kaufman, Barry Neil, *Happiness is a choice*, Random House, Sydney, 1991.

Kennedy, Gavin, *The perfect negotiation*, Century Business Random House, London, 1992.

Kidman, Antony, *Managing love and hate*, Biochemical and General Services, Australia, 1990.

Kübler-Ross, Elizabeth, *On death and dying*, Tavistock Publications, London, 1969.

Levy, S. M., Herberman, R. B., Lippman, M., et al., 'Immunological and psychological predictors of disease recurrence in patients with early stage breast cancer', *Behaviour Modification* 17, 1991.

Melville, Arabella & Johnson, Colin, *Cured to death*, Angus & Robertson, Sydney, 1982.

North, C. S., Clouse, R. E., Spitznagel, E. L., et al., 'The relation of ulcerative colitis to psychiatric factors: A review of findings and methods', *American Journal of Psychiatry* 147, 1990.

Pease, Alan, *Body language*, Camel, Sydney, 1981.

Readers Digest, *Encylopaedia of family health*, Readers Digest Association, Sydney, 1994.

Rossi, Ernest Lawrence, *The psychobiology of mindbody healing*, W. W. Norton and Comp. Inc., New York, 1986.

Rossi, Ernest & Cheek, David, *Mind-body therapy*, Norton, New York, 1988.

Scheinfeld, Amran, *Twins and super twins*, Pelican, London, 1973.

Schapiro, Francine, *Eye movement desensitisation and reprocessing*, Guildford Press, New York, 1995.

Silverstone, P. H., 'Depression increases mortality and morbidity in acute life-threatening medical illness', *Journal Psychosomatic Research*, 34, 1990.

Spiegal, David, *Living beyond limits*, Vermilion, Ebury Press, Random House, London, 1994.

Stoudemire, Alan, ed., *Psychological factors affecting medical conditions*, American Psychiatric Press Inc, London, 1995.

Yapku, Michael, *Suggestions of abuse*, Simon and Schuster, New York, 1994.

Zimbardo, Philip G., *Shyness*, Addison-Wesley Publishing Company, Sydney, 1977.